Fiancé  U.S.A!

A comprehensive walkthrough of the fiancé(e) visa (k-1) process

By Yuri & Bruce Brown

Fiancé(e) Visa to U.S.A!

Copyright © 2018 by YuriBruce

For information contact :

brucebrownftw@gmail.com

visaapproved.thinkific.com

Book and Cover design by YuriBruce

Acknowledgements

We would not have written this book without the continuous viewership and support of our online community. We have a very active community of international couples, immigrants, expats, content creators, and entrepreneurs that focus on helping each other out and lifting each other up.

Special thanks go out to the following YouTubers & Patrons:
T. Elliot, Chris / HT Logistics, Heath "instagator", The Big O. Experience, mamu, Ancient Alien's Andy, Jamal Waring, DanDanTheDrivingMan, Erick Sadler, KingPin, Emilio A., Darryl Charity, SciFi George, Tim H, Mike Angelo, David Thomas, Benjamin K., Art Carlson, JBarnes, Steve / Lina's World, William G., Chrdel10, Legsdiamond, EyeOnYouNews, James / Amores Del Caribe, Paul W., LucesRasmussen, juantwo, Matty Ghost, Geo Graphy, My Adventure in the Philippines, Chad W, Lily Petals, Robert F, Vyken Dalchau, TZ, Ken, Vivian (RIP), Michael Firestone, Derrick Floyd, Mrmiketman, Damion Asmond, Aida and Pano, Motor City Mad man.

Visa Approved Moderators:
Jessel and Todd Herrick, Kenneline Marie Romero, Ana Lou Niese, Jun C Spear, IAntonnette Abas Culbertson, Gracie Liner, Marj T., Anob Jagger, Jazie Lou Baron.

Other great people:
Debra Brown, C. Sincero (purpleshadow), Alyssa, Tori, and others that had our back from the beginning.
Let's keep it going YuribruceTeam!

Table of Contents

Thank you for buying this book!

As a big **thank you** for buying this book, we want to personally invite you to our Fiancé(e) Visa to USA! online course. This course contains a down and dirty video series of the material covered in this book and an audio version of this book, with downloadable sample templates of the supporting evidence.

Check it out at: *http://visaapproved.thinkific.com*

Also talk to us directly:

- facebook.com/yuribruceteam
- facebook.com/groups/k1visaAos
- http://youtube.com/yuribruceteam
- http://Yuribruce.com

Even though we are not immigration lawyers or authorized immigration consultants, we (or someone in our group going through the process) may be able to help.

No More Long-Distance Relationship!

Hey guys,

If you are currently in a long-distance relationship with your fiancé who lives in another country, you can get a K-1 fiancé visa to bring them to the U.S.A to be together. This book walks you through the fiancé visa process IN PLAIN ENGLISH.

We are Yuri and Bruce, an international couple who successfully went through this process years ago and have since shown 1000s of people what we did to end long-distance engagement using the K-1 visa. We did it with a 5 Step process that is in this book.

Step 1. I-129F Package
Walks the U.S. petitioner through the who, what, when and how of the fiancé application.
Step 2. National Visa Center
Transition the approved package from the USCIS to the embassy.
Step 3. Embassy Preparation
Helps the foreign fiancé gather all evidence and prepare for going to the embassy.
Step 4. Medical
What to expect in the U.S. immigration approved medical exam.
Step 5. Interview
Questions that they may ask in the K-1 fiancé visa interview at the embassy.

This book includes:

- Lessons and step by step instruction on the K-1 visa process in plain English
- Actual supporting evidence that was used for fiancé visa approval
- Where to find free resources to get more help through the process
- Bonus chapter: First steps to getting a conditional green card

We successfully got through the K-1 visa process in 2014. We did it as a team. We want to help you do the same. We did not have the money to go through an immigration lawyer and we just weren't sure about going through an authorized immigration consultant or agency. We are sure there are some good ones out there, but back then we had heard too many horror stories about them.

After going through the process, we decided to show others how we did it. We have been able to help 1000's of people over the years using the 5-step process detailed in this book.

We decided to put everything in one place (in this book and in companion audio, and video media – visaapproved.thinktific.com).

All the information on the K-1 visa is online for free, it is just all over the place. So, hunting all that information down while in a long-distance relationship can be very stressful. We have found that understanding the K-1 visa process and working as a team is very helpful.

YOU CAN DO IT!

Disclaimer

Before we start we want to be clear that we are not immigration lawyers or "authorized" immigration consultants. We are just normal people like you who want to share what we know about the process. All the information we provide is from government resources, our personal experience, and the experience of 1000's of others over the years.

There are some cases where the U.S. petitioner & foreign fiancé(e) may need an immigration lawyer. This information is not a replacement for an authorized consultant or an immigration lawyer if it is needed. Even with an authorized consultant or immigration lawyer, this information can still help the applicant understand the process. We decided to put everything we learned into one place and this is it.

Please understand that we cannot guarantee success because each case is different, neither can a lawyer or authorized consultant. Ultimately, the process depends on the interaction between the petitioner, the foreign fiancé(e), and the U.S. government.

Our goal here is to empower the applicants by giving a simplified step by step view of the process. Pay very close attention to the requirements of the K-1 visa process.

The U.S. petitioner and foreign fiancé(e) can also talk to us directly:

- https://www.facebook.com/yuribruceteam
- https://facebook.com/groups/k1visaAos   (our   Visa Approved! group)
- **http://visaapproved.thinktific.com**
- Email: brucebrownftw@gmail.com

What is the K-1 Fiancé(e) Visa?

According to the U.S. Citizenship and Immigration Services (USCIS), *"The K-1 is a nonimmigrant visa that permits a foreign national fiancé(e) of a U.S. citizen to travel to the United States to marry the petitioning U.S. citizen sponsor within 90 days of admission to the country."*

Basic Information and Requirements of the K-1:

- **Summary of the Entire K-1 Process.** The U.S. citizen "petitions" their foreign fiancé(e) "beneficiary" with a Form I-129F, Petition for Alien Fiancé(e) and sends it to the USCIS along with the fee (a check or money order) and supporting documents.
  - USCIS conducts a background check on petitioner
  - Once approved, the USCIS sends the I-129F packages to the Department of State, National Visa Center (NVC), who sends it to the applicable embassy
  - The embassy contacts the foreign fiancé(e) and tells them to gather the required documents, gets a medical exam for an interview with the U.S. embassy consular officer (CO)
  - If the CO approves, the K-1 visa is placed inside the passport of the foreign fiancé(e) and they can use that to enter the U.S. one time in order to get married within 90 days of entering the U.S.
- **Bringing Children of the Foreign Fiancé(e)**. The K-1 process also allows the U.S. citizen to bring the children of the foreign fiancé(e) to the USA under the K-2 VISA. The child of the foreign fiancé(e) must be unmarried and under 21 years of age.
- **K-1 Requirements:**

- ❑ *MAKE SURE* the U.S. citizen (petitioner) and the foreign fiancé(e) (beneficiary) are **legally able to marry.** This means that the foreign fiancé(e) and petitioner are both either single, divorced/annulled or a widow(er). If either of them is divorced/annulled or widowed, they need to provide evidence.
- ❑ **Petitioner & foreign fiancé(e) MUST physically meet in person** and should have pictures together. The meeting should have been within 2 years of filing.
- ❑ **Poverty guideline.** During the foreign fiancé(e)'s embassy interview, they have to prove that the U.S. petitioner makes enough money to support the foreign fiancé(e) in the USA. The U.S. petitioner's income must be above the poverty line. If the U.S. petitioner does not make enough income, they may have other options (discussed later in this book).

More on Meeting in Person and the Exceptions

Before the U.S. petitioner files, they must have met the foreign fiancé(e) in person at least once within the last 2 years. Please note that this does not mean that the relationship is 2 years old. There is no rule for how long the relationship should be. There are couples that have only known each other for 6 months or less and they are successful with the K-1 process. But there is a rule for physically meeting in person and that must happen at least once within the last 2 years before the U.S. petitioner files the I-129F.

There are only (2) exceptions to the rule of meeting physically in person:

> **(1) Religion/Traditions.** The requirement for the U.S. petitioner to meet the fiancé(e) in person would violate strict and long-established customs of the fiancé(e)'s culture or social practice, and that all aspects of the traditional arrangements have been or will be met in accordance with the custom or practice.
>
> **(2) Extreme Hardships.** The requirement for the U.S. petitioner to meet the fiancé(e) in person would result in extreme hardship to the petitioner.

NOTE: Based on what we have seen, these exceptions seem to be hard to get. We don't know anyone that got around the rule of meeting in person.

Beyond the K-1 Visa and After Marriage

After marriage, the K-1 visa holder fills out the I-485, adjustment of status:

- This allows the foreign fiancé(e) to change their status from temporary nonimmigrant to an immigrant with a 2-year conditional green card.
- Becoming a green card holder allows the immigrant to eventually become a U.S. citizen if they want. Or they can just keep renewing the green card.

The 5 Steps of the *Fiancé(e) Visa to U.S.A!*

The *Fiancé(e) Visa to U.S.A!* method breaks the entire K-1 process up into 5 steps. We did this to make the fiancé(e) visa (K-1) process easier to understand and it gives the U.S. petitioner and foreign fiancé(e) goals and tasks they can reach together. This book goes into detail for each step. Here are the steps that will be addressed in this book:

5 Steps of the Fiancé(e) to U.S.A

Step 1 - Petition Package

- Explains the K-1 is and who it is for
- Walks the applicant through the required data on the I-129F, Petition for Alien fiancé(e) form
- Explains all the supporting evidence that goes with the I-129F package

Step 2 - National Visa Center

- After approval of the I-129F, Petition for Alien fiancé(e), the USCIS will send the package to the National Visa Center (NVC)
- What is the NVC and how do you contact them?
- How do you check the status of a case?
- We talk about what the U.S. petitioner needs to do once the I-129F package is with the NVC

Step 3 - Embassy Preparation

- What does the foreign fiancé(e) need to do next?
- Where do they need to go?
- What documents do they need to prepare?
- Setting up the interview

Step 4 - Medical Preparation

- What does the foreign fiancé(e) need to do for the medical exam?
- Where do they need to go to get the medical exam?
- Where to find more information on the medical exam?
- What to expect with the medical exam?

Step 5 - Interview

- What is the interview like?
- Commonly asked questions of the interview

Bonus: *What do you do after the K-1 and after marriage?*

Introduction Reference:

"Visas for Fiancé(e)s of U.S. Citizens." USCIS, 5 May 2018, https://www.uscis.gov/family/family-us-citizens/visas-fiancees-us-citizens

"Nonimmigrant Visa for a Fiancé(e) (K-1)." U.S. Department of State - Bureau of Consular Affairs, 9 May 2018 https://travel.state.gov/content/travel/en/us-visas/immigrate/family-immigration/nonimmigrant-visa-for-a-fiance-k-1.html

"Form I-129F Instructions." USCIS, 5 May 2018, https://www.uscis.gov/sites/default/files/files/form/i-129finstr.pdf

"Poverty Guidelines." Office of The Assistant Secretary for Planning and Evaluation (ASPE), 5 May 2018, https://aspe.hhs.gov/poverty-guidelines

"What is the difference between an Immigrant Visa vs. Nonimmigrant Visa?" U.S. Customs and Border Protection, 5 May 2018, https://help.cbp.gov

Step 1. Petition Package
Step 1.0 Petition Package Overview

Welcome to Step 1. Petition Package! This step will walk the petitioner through the first form they need to fill out called Form I-129F, Petition for Alien Fiancé(e):

- https://www.uscis.gov/i-129f

I-129F Petition Package Checklist:

I-129F Supporting Evidence Checklist	
Tasks/Documents	
Have a REAL Relationship & Get Engaged. There is no restriction on the length of time the couple should be together. But it is important that the relationship be real, not just from a legal perspective, but also for the sake of the couple. The couple must be engaged.	
A Photocopy of the U.S. Petitioner's Birth Certificate (or naturalization document). A photocopy of the U.S. petitioner's birth certificate or naturalization document to prove U.S. citizenship.	
Copies of Court or Arrest Record (if applicable). U.S. petitioners who have been arrested, charged, or convicted of a crime must present copies or transcripts of court or arrest records relating to the crime or offense *(see "Criminal Information")*.	
Letters of Intent to Marry. Letters stating the petitioner and foreign fiancé(e)'s intention to marry each other upon the fiancé(e)'s arrival to the USA. Both documents must be signed or one letter signed by both.	
Proof of Meeting. The U.S. petitioner must provide evidence that they physically met the foreign fiancé(e) in person within two years of submitting the I-129F package. This evidence could include (but should not be limited to) pictures together, tickets and receipts with names, locations, and dates.	
Declaration of How We Met. A statement from the U.S. petitioner explaining how, when, where and why they met the foreign fiancé(e). This statement should be signed and match the proof of meeting dates and locations.	
A Certified Copy of Proof of Termination of a Prior Marriage. If applicable, official documents (divorce decree, annulment decree, or death certificate, etc.) that prove all prior marriages contracted by the foreign fiancé(e) and the petitioner have been legally terminated prior to the I-129F.	
Passport Style. Get a passport style photo. Write the name of the U.S. petitioner on the back of the passport style photo.	
Legal Name Change (if applicable). If the U.S. petitioner or foreign fiancé(e) goes by any other documented names, provide evidence of the other names (previous marriages/divorces, or legal name change documents).	
Cover Letter / G-1145 (Optional). A cover letter to the I-129F package works as a table of contents for all the items in the package. The cover letter will be the top page of the package. The G-1145 is an e-	

When the U.S. petitioner has completed the application and gathered all required documents, they will submit the package to the United States Citizenship and Immigration Services (USCIS).

File Form I-129F at the USCIS Dallas Lockbox facility

For U.S. Postal Service (USPS):

USCIS
P.O. Box 660151
Dallas, TX 75266

For FedEx, UPS, and DHL deliveries:
USCIS
Attn: I-129F
2501 South State Highway 121 Business
Suite 400
Lewisville, TX 75067

cover (optional)

G1145 notification (optional)

passport pic

legal name change

intent to marry

proof of meeting

declaration how met

naturalization cert

divorce decree

Birth Certificate

USCIS payment

I-129f

Figure, I-129F Tree

When the U.S. petitioner is ready to send the documents, the envelope should be a thick packet. One misconception of the I-129f, Petition for Alien Fiancé(e) is that it is just one form and a fee. In truth, the I-129F package is like a tree with many branches of required documents (Figure, I-129F Tree).

In Step 1 of the fiancé(e) visa to USA process, we will walk the U.S. petitioner through the first part of the K-1 fiancé(e) visa process. The U.S. petitioner will need some help from the foreign fiancé(e) but most of Step 1 is done by the petitioner.

Step 1.1 Petition Package: Fill out Form I-129F

Step 1.1 of the Fiancé(e) Visa to USA walks the petitioner through the Form I-129F, Petition for Alien Fiancé(e). The purpose of Form I-129F is to classify the alien fiancé(e) as a K-1 nonimmigrant so they may enter the United States to marry the U.S. petitioner. It also allows the foreign fiancé(e) to pursue an adjustment of status to become a U.S. immigrant and get a permanent resident card (green card).

K-2, Children of the Foreign Fiancé(e)

The children of the foreign fiancé(e) who become a K-1 visa holder may obtain a nonimmigrant visa to accompany the foreign fiancé(e) into the USA. *The U.S. petitioner adds the child or children to the I-129F petition where indicated by the form. Although there is only one initial I-129F filing fee for the foreign fiancé(e) and children, there will be additional costs with the visa fee and medical fee later in the process.* The children of the K-1 are classified as K-2 nonimmigrants. The children must be unmarried and under 21 years old.

> *NOTE: What are K-3 and K-4?*
> *K-3 is a nonimmigrant spousal visa that allows the foreign wife or husband to come to the U.S. and apply for a conditional green card. K-4 is for the children of K-3 nonimmigrant. Form I-129F is also used by K-3/K-4, but the process has some differences (K-3/K-4 are not covered in this book).*

Plan to Organize and Keep Copies

Before the petitioner and the foreign fiancé(e) do anything with the I-129F, they should plan out how they are going to organize all documentation. The petitioner & foreign fiancé(e) will need to keep copies for themselves. We recommend keeping digital copies of everything in organized folders and categorized where it can be protected and shared by both the petitioner and foreign fiancé(e).

Getting digital copies can be done by scanning (or taking pictures) of all documents and evidence before sending them to the government. Scan them and save them to the hard drive, to a flash drive, or to a cloud service. Instead of scanning, the petitioner can also take a photo of each document and keep them on a mobile device. Just make sure it is a very clear picture of each document with a high resolution because they will need to be printed out later. These digital copies can also be encrypted or password protected by using free applications such as .zip or .rar software.

When printing a hard copy, make at least three copies of all forms, documents, and evidence:

- (1) For the U.S. Petitioner
- (1) For the foreign fiancé(e)
- (1) To send to the government

Organize all the documents and put them in a safe place.

Original Documents

Most of the evidence can be copies for the I-129F. The only thing that must be original is a recent passport style photo of the petitioner and beneficiary and the check or money order for payment of the fee.

In some cases, during the process, the U.S. government will specifically request original copies. When ordering original documents (such as birth certificates for the foreign fiancé(e) needed for the U.S. embassy in Step 3) try to get 3 or 4 of the original. Many of the forms, documents, and evidence will be needed again throughout the process.

Get the Form I-129F, Petition for Alien Fiancé(e)

The petitioner can get the most current Form I-129F on the USCIS.gov site:

- https://www.uscis.gov/i-129f
- https://www.uscis.gov/forms
- https://www.uscis.gov/forms/order-forms-mail-or-phone

If they cannot download the form, the petitioner can order the I-129F and other forms by phone: **1-800-870-3676**

The petitioner can also do mail order for the I-129F by going to the following site: https://egov.uscis.gov/formsbymail/

Avoid Using Expired Versions of the Forms

Always make sure the most current version of the form is being used. The government forms expire often. Go to the following site to check the latest updates on any visa form:

- https://www.uscis.gov/forms-updates

In order to check to see if the form is expired, look on the top right-hand corner of the form (Figure, I-129F Expired). We know of people who have had to re-submit forms because the one they sent was expired.

Figure, Expired I-129F

I-129F: Edit PDF Files or Write with Black Ink

When the petitioner fills out the document, they can download the PDF to type in responses or print out the Form I-129F and write responses in using black ink. There are many free applications online that allow the user to edit to a PDF file. One example is Acrobat Pro (free trial).

How to Edit PDF Files:

1. Open a file in Acrobat (use trial version Acrobat Pro).
2. Click on the Edit PDF tool in the right pane.
3. Click the text or image you wish to edit. Acrobat shows you the tools you'll need.
4. Add or edit text on the page. Lines and paragraphs reflow automatically, or you can click and drag to resize elements.
5. Add, replace, move, or resize images on the page using selections from the Objects list.
6. Click on the Link, Headers, Footers, Watermark, or Background tool to edit your PDF further.

Another way to edit is to upload the PDF into an online PDF editor. You can find these online for free.

Whether filling the form out, printing with black ink or typing make sure you answer all questions fully and accurately. With questions that do not apply, the petitioner can type or print "N/A". If a numerical response is zero or none, type or print "None".

Top and Bottom of I-129F & Extra Space On I-129F

The last part of the form is for extra space. If the applicant needs extra space, they can use the last part of the Form I-129F. The last part is for "Additional Information" that can be attached to the I-129F package. The applicant can print more pages of "Additional Information" or use separate white printer pages. Additional pages need the petitioner's name or Alien Number (if any) at the top of the form.

The top section of the Form I-129F is "For USCIS Use Only". Don't mark this area and don't worry about it.

Figure, For USCIS Use Only before and after

The USCIS uses this top portion to track the I-129F package as it is moved from one government agency to another and turned into a "case". They determine if the fee was paid if there was an *"Extraordinary Circumstance Waiver"*, and they make notes for other government workers handling the case.

Part 1. Information About You

The first thing the applicant needs to fill out is the Alien Registration Number, USCIS Online Account Number, and U.S. Social Security Number. This applies to the U.S. petitioner who is requesting their foreign fiancé(e).

Alien Registration Number (if applicable)

On this part of the form, the alien registration (A-number) only applied to the U.S. petitioner if they are a naturalized U.S. citizen (citizens born as foreign nationals, immigrated to the U.S. and legally became citizens). *If this does not apply to the petitioner, then they don't need to worry about it.* Petitioners who are naturalized citizens have an A-Number in their immigrant records. That number is on their USCIS account or they can find this number on documents from one of the following: Immigration and Customs Enforcement (ICE), Customs and Border Protection (CBP), the Department of Justice (DOJ), Department of States (DOS) or Executive Office for Immigration Review.

USCIS Online Account Number (if applicable)

If the petitioner has this number, they should provide it. USCIS Online Account Number is for people who have filed a petition with the USCIS in the past. You can find this number by logging into the USCIS site. USCIS Online Account number was previously called USCIS Electronic Immigration System (USCIS ELIS). **This is NOT the same as an A-Number.**

Social Security Number

The USCIS will need the petitioner's Social Security Number (SSN) (if any) to fully identify who they are. This also allows them to conduct a background check on the petitioner.

129F Items

On the Form I-129F, the petitioner must identify the classification of the form. The I-129F can be used for a spousal nonimmigrant visa (K-3) or fiancé(e) nonimmigrant visa (K-1). Select the box that indicates whether the U.S. petitioner is filing for a fiancé(e) (K-1) or a spouse (K-3). If they are filing for a spousal visa (K-3), indicate whether the Form I-130 was filed on that beneficiary's behalf. *The spousal visa process is not covered in this book.*

U.S. Petitioner's Full Name. In this section, the petitioner will need to fill in their Last Name, First Name and Middle Name (in that order).

Other Names. If the petitioner has ever used other names, including aliases, maiden names, nicknames then they will need to provide them in "Other Names". What they mean are names that the petitioner goes by on other official documents such as marriage, social security, or name change documents. If extra space is needed, they can provide them in the "Additional Information" portion on the I-129F.

Petitioner's Mailing Address. Provide the address where the petitioner would like to receive written correspondence regarding this petition's status (i.e. notice of action letters). Indicate whether the mailing address is the same as the place where the petitioner resides (physical address).

NOTE for Petitioners Living Abroad. Some U.S. petitioners who are still abroad when they file the I-129F provide the physical address that they will be living in the US, with the understanding that they will be back in the USA before any mail gets back from the USCIS or have the mail forwarded to their address abroad. If they do not have an address in the USA, they sometimes use a relative's or friend's address temporarily until they get their own mailing address in the US. The form allows the petitioner to put a physical address that is different from the mailing address that is abroad. The petitioner can live abroad until the foreign fiancé(e) is approved.

Eventually, the K-1 process requires that the petitioner and foreign fiancé(e) be able to prove that they are domiciled (living in) the USA. If the petitioner has no intention of living in the USA with their future wife for a long period of time, then they may not need a K-1 visa because the K-1 is specifically to allow the foreign fiancé(e) to come to the USA, get married, and get a legal permanent residency (green card) to legally stay with their spouse in the USA.

Petitioner's Address History. Provide the addresses of the places the petitioner has resided in the last five years. If more space is needed, the petitioner can use the "Additional Information" pages at the end of the I-129F form or attach a separate sheet of paper. On the separate sheet of paper type or print the petitioner's name and A-Number (if any) at the top of each sheet; indicate the Page Number and Item Number to which the answer refers, and sign and date each sheet.

Petitioner's Employment History. Provide the names and addresses of the petitioner's employers, occupations, and the dates of employment for the jobs held over the last five years.

Petitioner's Gender. Indicate whether the petitioner is male or female.

Petitioner's Date of Birth. Provide the petitioner's date of birth in mm/dd/yyyy format.

Petitioner's Marital Status. Indicate the petitioner's current marital status. The petitioner cannot be married while filing the K-1 visa.

Petitioner's Place of Birth. Provide the name of the city or town, province/state, and country where the petitioner was born.

Information About Petitioner's Parents. Provide each of the petitioner's parents' full names, dates of birth, places of birth, and current cities/town/villages and countries of residence. If the petitioner does not know a parent's information, print or type "UNKNOWN".

Name of Petitioner's Previous Spouse(s). Indicate whether the petitioner has been previously married. If the answer is "Yes," provide the full names of each previous spouse and the date that each marriage ended. If the petitioner has had more than one previous spouse, use the "Additional Information" part of the I-129F or a blank sheet for the additional ex-spouses. If the petitioner has been previously married, they must provide evidence that ALL previous marriages have ended (divorce decree, annulment, or death certificate). The I-129F must be filed AFTER the date that the previous marriage ended. If the petitioner is divorced/annulled or a widow(er), the government will look at the date the previous marriages ended and the evidence that must be provided. This is explained in further detail in this book.

Petitioner's Citizenship Information. Select the box that describes how the petitioner obtained their U.S. citizenship. Indicate whether they obtained a Certificate of Naturalization or a Certificate of Citizenship and provide the date and place the document was issued. The U.S. petitioner will have to provide a copy of the U.S. birth certificate or naturalization documents along with certificate number and place of issuance.

Petitioner's Previous Filings. Indicate whether the petitioner has ever filed another Form I-129F for any other spouse or fiancé(e). If the response is "Yes," provide that person's full name and the person's A-Number (if any). Provide the date the petition was filed and the final action taken (for example, petition approved, denied, revoked, or withdrawn). If the petitioner has filed for more than one previous spouse or fiancé(e), use "Additional Information" to respond to these questions for each beneficiary or attach a separate sheet of paper. On the separate sheet of paper type or print the petitioner's name and A-Number (if any) at the top of each sheet, indicate the Page Number and Item Number to which the answer refers, and sign and date each sheet.

Age of Petitioner's Children. Indicate whether the petitioner has any children under 18 years of age. If the answer is "Yes," provide the age for each of the petitioner's children under 18 years of age. If the applicant needs extra space to complete this section, use the space provided in the "Additional Information" part of I-129F.

Places the Petitioner Has Resided. Provide all the U.S. states and foreign countries which the petitioner has resided since reaching 18 years of age. Use the "Additional Information" portion of the I-129F for extra space.

Part 2. Information About Your Beneficiary

Part 2 of the Form I-129F focuses on the foreign fiancé(e) (also known as a "beneficiary") and their children, if any, are coming with the foreign fiancé(e). The petitioner should list all the foreign fiancé(e) children even if they are not going to be coming to the U.S. on a K-2 visa.

Part 2 - I-129F Items Include:

Foreign Fiancé(e)'s Full Name. Provide the beneficiary's full legal name. The foreign fiancé(e)'s name should be written in the Roman alphabet. This means the English alphabet must be used. This is important to note for some fiancé(e)s whose names have never been written in English. (For example, countries that do not use Romanized alphabets like China, Thailand, and Japan.)

U.S. Social Security Number (SSN). In most cases, the foreign fiancé(e) will not have a social security number, but if they do then provide it.

A-Number. If the foreign fiancé(e) has an A-Number (alien number) then provide it. The beneficiary may have an A-Number if they have had immigration records. The beneficiary can find this number on documents he or she received from USCIS, ICE, CBP, EOIR, or DOS.

Date of Birth. Provide the beneficiary's date of birth in mm/dd/yyyy format.

Gender. Indicate whether the beneficiary is male or female.

Marital Status. Indicate the beneficiary's current marital status. The beneficiary must be available to marry.

Place of Birth. Provide the name of the city or town, province or state, and country where the beneficiary was born. This should be written in the Roman alphabet.

Other Names. If the foreign fiancé(e) has ever used other names, including aliases, maiden names, and nicknames provide them. Provide evidence of the previous names (marriage certificate & name change forms).

Mailing Address of the Beneficiary. Provide the beneficiary's current mailing address.

Beneficiary's Address History. Provide the addresses for the places the foreign fiancé(e) has resided in the last five years. Use the "Additional Information" sheets in the I-129F if more space is needed. Or attach a separate sheet of paper. On the separate sheet of paper type or print the petitioner's name and A-Number (if any) at the top of each sheet, indicate the Page Number and Item Number to which the answer refers, and sign and date each sheet.

Beneficiary's Employment History. Provide the names and addresses of the beneficiary's employers, occupations, and the dates of employment for the jobs the beneficiary has held over the last five years.

Information About the Beneficiary's Parents. Provide each of the beneficiary's parents' full names, dates of birth, places of birth, and current cities and countries of residence. If the parents of the beneficiary are unknown, type or print "UNKNOWN".

Name of the Previous Spouse. Indicate whether the foreign fiancé(e) has ever been previously married. If the answer is "Yes," provide the full name of the beneficiary's previous spouse(s) and the date that each marriage ended. If the beneficiary has more than one previous spouse, use the space provided in "Additional Information" section to respond to questions for each spouse. If they were previously married, they will have to provide evidence that the previous marriage ended (annulment, divorce, or death certificate).

Form I-94 Arrival-Departure Record (If applicable). Select the box to indicate whether the foreign fiancé(e) has ever been in the United States. Provide the date of the beneficiary's most recent entry in the United States, his or her I-94 Arrival-Departure Record Number, if available, and his or her immigration status at the time of arrival (for example, student, tourist, temporary worker, without inspection). Provide the expiration date and identification numbers on the I-94 or I-95 Arrival-Departure Records, travel documents, and or passports. If there are no arrival or I-94 expiration, print or type "N/A".

NOTE: If the beneficiary was admitted to the United States by CBP at an airport or seaport after April 30, 2013, he or she may have been issued an electronic Form I-94 by CBP, instead of a paper Form I-94. The beneficiary may visit the CBP website at www.cbp.gov/i94 to obtain a paper version of an electronic Form I-94.

Passport or Travel Document Number. Type or print that passport or travel document number in Part 2 of the I-129F. The passport number is on the information page of the passport. If there is a different kind of travel document, provide the number on that travel document. Provide the country of issuance for the passport or travel document.

Children of Beneficiary. Indicate whether the foreign fiancé(e) has any children. If the answer is "Yes," provide information about each child of the foreign fiancé(e). Include the child's full name, country of birth, and date of birth. If the child resides at a different address than the foreign fiancé(e), provide the address where the child currently resides. If the foreign fiancé(e) has many children, use the "Additional Information" part of the I-129F for more space or attach a separate sheet of paper. On the separate sheet of paper type or print the petitioner's name and A-Number (if any) at the top of each sheet, indicate the Page Number and Item Number to which the answer refers, and sign and date each sheet.

Address in the United States Where the Beneficiary Intends to Live. Provide the address and daytime telephone number where the foreign fiancé(e) intends to live when he/she arrives in the United States. This is usually the physical address of the U.S. petitioner.

The Beneficiary's Physical Address Abroad. Provide the address and daytime telephone number where the foreign fiancé(e) currently resides abroad. If the foreign fiancé(e) works abroad, they can usually still process the visa through the local U.S. embassy.

NOTE on the address abroad: During the U.S. embassy interview, the foreign fiancé(e) will have to provide a police clearance from that country and other countries that they worked in for 6 months or more (see Step 3 for more details).

The Beneficiary's Name and Address in His or Her Native Alphabet. If the foreign fiancé(e)s native writing does not use Roman letters (examples, Chinese, Thai, Russian) provide his or her name and physical address abroad in the native alphabet.

Is the beneficiary Related to the Petitioner? Indicate whether the U.S. petitioner and the foreign fiancé(e) have a familial relationship and if so, describe the nature and degree of relationship (for example, second cousins, maternal aunt or uncle). Select "N/A" if the beneficiary is the spouse of the petitioner.

Meeting in Person Requirement

Part 2 of the I-129F asks if, *"you and your fiancé(e) have met in person during the two years before filing this petition?"*

If the answer is "Yes": Describe the circumstances of the in-person meeting. Attach evidence to demonstrate that the petitioner and foreign fiancé(e) were in each other's physical presence within the required two-year period before filing. This can be explained in a "declaration of how we met" (described in Step 1.2) or on the space provided in the "Additional Information" part of the I-129F. The U.S. petitioner should also provide evidence of meeting in person (described in Step 1.3).

If the answer is "No": Explain in detail any reasons the petitioner and foreign fiancé(e) may have for requesting an exemption from the requirement. The petitioner must request a waiver and demonstrate that meeting in person would have pose an extreme hardship or violated strict and long-established customs of the foreign fiancé(e)'s culture or social practice and that all aspects of the traditional arrangements have been or will be met in accordance with the custom or practice.

Include evidence to support the claim. Create a letter that explains why the petitioner and foreign fiancé(e) have not met. And how they are abiding by customs. Or how the extreme hardship makes it impossible to visit in person. The letter should be signed and accompanied by evidence. The evidence may include things like:

- medical records with a statement from a doctor
- statements from religious leaders
- evidence of immediate danger

NOTE: In the years that we have been talking to 1000's of petitioners and foreign fiancé(e)s, **we have never seen this work.**

What is an International Marriage Broker (IMB)

The USCIS wants to know if the U.S. petitioner and the foreign fiancé(e) met through an international marriage broker service. You may have heard the term "mail order bride" service which is seen by some as a negative term. The correct name is international marriage broker. There is some overlap between what a "dating site" is and what an "international marriage broker" is but they are not the same thing.

The term "international marriage broker" (IMB) refers to an organization or individual that charges fees to provide dating, matrimonial, or matchmaking services, or provides social referrals between U.S. citizens/lawful permanent residents and foreign national clients by providing personal contact information or otherwise facilitating communication between individuals.

Here are some reasons why IMBs are NOT dating sites:

1. The person or organization offers services to every country, nationality, and gender (dating sites are for everyone).
2. The person or organization's services are not just U.S. citizens connecting with foreign nationals (dating sites can be two people from the same country).
3. The person or organization's matchmaking is based on cultural/religious traditions for non-profit (some dating sites focus on religion).

Most dating sites offer services to everyone regardless of nationality and gender so they do not qualify as IMBs. IMBs are also not for connecting couples from the same country. Most dating sites cater to people within their own country as well as the international community.

Request for Evidence IMB - Tell them it is NOT an IMB

Sometimes the USCIS mistakes dating sites mentioned by the U.S. petitioner for international marriage brokers. When this happens, the USCIS sends a request for more evidence (RFE) notice of action. This is a letter from the USCIS stating that they need a certain document or evidence. In the case of the IMB RFE, they want the IMB's name, organization name, website, mailing address, and daytime telephone number in the I-129F documentation.

If you want to talk about the dating site, Explain it

In order to avoid this, the petitioner needs to explain what the dating site is. Describe what type of dating site it is, the circumstance of initially meeting on the dating site, and maybe explain that you continued to develop your relationship OFF the dating site. The USCIS needs to understand that the dating site is NOT an IMB because it services many nationalities and countries and it not restricted by gender. For example, the site's service does not just focus on ONLY men from America looking for ONLY marriage to single women from Thailand and/or Ukraine. Dating sites typically allow men and women to sign-up from anywhere in the world to meet other men and women for dating, marriage or even just for fun. So, dating sites do not classify as IMBs.

Don't Mention Dating Sites, Just Say "ONLINE"

Another option is *DO NOT mention that you met on a dating site*. It will just confuse them, especially if you don't explain the site and how you met there. Just say you initially "met online" and focus on how you met in person and developed a relationship within the last two years of filing. If you do mention the name of the dating site the petitioner must explain that it is NOT an international marriage broker site, because if you don't explain it, they have to assume it was an IMB to comply with U.S. laws that are designed to protect the foreign fiancé(e).

The IMB RFE letter from the USCIS looks like this:

"You stated you met your fiancé(e) through an online dating website; however, you did not provide any specific detail about this website. Submit information about this website and the circumstances under which you and your beneficiary met to establish the relationship.

The evidence submitted indicates that you may have met the beneficiary through the services of an international marriage broker (IMB). You stated you met the beneficiary through a dating website. Although the answer to question X on the fiancé(e) petition indicates that you did not meet the beneficiary through the services of an international marriage broker, you did not specify that the website is not an international marriage broker as defined by regulations. An International Marriage Broker is considered a business that charges fees for dating, matrimonial, matchmaking services, or social referrals between United States citizens and foreign nationals. As such, you must submit a copy of the signed written consent form that the International Marriage Broker obtained from the beneficiary authorizing the release of his personal contact information to you, or documentation to establish that the website is not an international marriage broker."

If they receive this RFE, the U.S. petitioner can reply to the USCIS with evidence that the dating site mentioned is not an international marriage broker. For evidence, go to the website and obtain the Terms of Service.

In some cases, the TOS will state that they are NOT an IMB. The petitioner can also get an email response that explains that the dating site is NOT an IMB. If the dating site has "IMB services", the petitioner can explain that they did not use those services and the relationship was developed in person. Here is an example of Terms of Service the U.S. petitioner can send the USCIS:

Australia
Email: team@FilipinoCupid.com
Fax Number: + 61 7 3103 4000

2.13 Name, Address, Email & Fax (German Residents Only)

The User may deliver notice of their termination using the contact form available at all the Company's websites, or by sending an email, fax or letter to the Company. The fax number and email address of the Company are sent to the User upon registration and appear at clause 2.12(b) above in these Terms of Use.

2.14 Consequences of Withdrawal (German Residents Only)

In the event of termination in accordance with clause 2.12, the Company and the User shall be obliged to restore any benefits received or gains (including interest). If the User is unable or partially unable to restore the benefits, or only able to restore them an unsatisfactory manner then the User must reimburse the Company for the corresponding value. The User must fulfil its obligations to reimburse within 30 days of giving notice of their termination. The User's right of termination under other sections of these Terms of Use shall not be affected by the User's cancellation right under this clause.

2.15 Lapse of Right to Terminate (German Residents Only)

In accordance with § 312d Par. 3 BGB (German Civil Code), the User's right of termination in clause 2.12 will lapse prior to the two week period if.

(a) The Company has begun performing the services for which the User is registered with the express consent of the User; or

(b) the User has initiated the services for which the User is registered including accessing the services relevant to the membership chosen by the User at registration.

3. The Service

The Service is an internet information service that facilitates contact between members who may or may not be seeking friendship or a relationship. It is not a marriage brokering service, mail order bride service or a matchmaking service. The Company is under no obligation to broker any other member or members for you.

4.1 Own risk

You acknowledge that your use of the Service and the Website is solely at your own risk.

Figure,   RFE   IMB   –   Send   Dating   Site   Term   of   Services

35

International Marriage Broker Regulation Act (IMBRA)

Since international marriage brokers connect couples so fast, the U.S. government wants to make sure the foreign fiancé(e) is safe. Because some come to the U.S. and end up being with someone who abuses them (or worse), the U.S. government came up with the International Marriage Broker Regulation Act.

Under the International Marriage Broker Regulation Act (IMBRA), U.S. citizen petitioners are required to disclose information on any permanent protection or restraining order (civil or criminal) related to any specified crime described in Part 3. of these instructions, and information on any convictions for any specified crime described in Part 3. In addition, IMBRA requires USCIS to maintain a database to track multiple Form I-129Fs filed by the same petitioner. USCIS will notify petitioners upon approval of a second Form I-129F petition they filed and that their information has been entered into a multiple-visa petition tracking database. USCIS will enter into this database all additional Form I-129Fs that the petitioner files.

International Marriage Broker (IMB) Information. Indicate whether the petitioner met the beneficiary through the service of an IMB. If the response is "Yes," provide the IMB's name, organization name, website, mailing address, and daytime telephone number.

U.S. Embassy or U.S. Consulate Requested

The petitioner must provide the city or town and country of the U.S. embassy or U.S. consulate where the foreign fiancé(e) will apply for his or her visa.

It is best to choose the U.S. embassy where the foreign fiancé(e) currently lives. For example, if the foreign fiancé(e) is working abroad and they will be there throughout the K-1 visa process, they need to choose the U.S. embassy in the country they are working in. However, if the foreign fiancé(e) is working abroad but planning to move back to their home country in the middle of the K-1 Visa process, they should figure out where they will be when the embassy interview takes place.   The petitioner and foreign fiancé(e) may also need to do a little research to determine what embassy near them actually do visas. The U.S. embassy that does visas is usually in big cities or the capital of the country. U.S. consulates may be closer, but not all consulates do visas. For example, Yuri (foreign fiancé(e)) is from Cebu City, Philippines. Although there is a U.S. Consulate Agency in Cebu, only the U.S. Embassy in Manila, Philippines does visas, so she had to travel to Manila to do the interview (and medical exam which we will talk about in Step 4).

NOTE: In some cases, the petitioner and foreign fiancé(e) have to choose a U.S. embassy outside the country that the foreign fiancé(e) is currently living in. In this situation, the U.S. embassy may not accept the case. Acceptance is at the discretion of the U.S. embassy.

Part 3. Other Information

One of the most important portions of the I-129F is the criminal information. If the petitioner has no arrests, no convictions, and just some traffic tickets, then this section is very easy. If the petitioner has been arrested or convicted of serious crimes, then this helps the USCIS to conduct a background check and gives the petitioner a chance to tell their side of the story.

Criminal Information

This section will ask questions to allow the petitioner to indicate whether they have ever been the subject of a temporary or permanent protection order or restraining order (either civil or criminal) related to any of the crimes specified, arrested, or convicted of any of the crimes specified.
If they were ever arrested or convicted of any of the specified crimes (in the questions on the I-129F), they must submit certified copies of all court and police records showing the charges and disposition for every arrest or conviction. This must be done even if the records were sealed, expunged, or otherwise cleared, and regardless of whether anyone, including a judge, law enforcement officer, or attorney, informed the petitioner that they no longer have a criminal record. The I-129F criminal information questions include (but are not limited to):

- Have you ever been subject to a temporary or permanent protection or restraining order (either civil or criminal)?
- Have you ever been arrested or convicted of any of the following crimes?

The focus is on specific kinds of crimes.

Specific Crimes and What I-129F Focuses On

USCIS is trying to determine if the foreign fiancé(e) will be safe with the U.S. petitioner by looking at specific types of crimes the petitioner has committed:

> **A. Convictions for domestic violence** (including felony or misdemeanor of violence committed by a person), sexual assault, child abuse or child neglect, dating violence, elder abuse, and stalking or an attempt to commit any such crime:
>
> > (1) Who is a current or former spouse of the victim
> > (2) With whom the victim shares a child in common
> > (3) Who is cohabitating with or has cohabitated with the victim
> > (4) Who is similarly situated to a spouse of the victim under the domestic family violence laws of the relevant jurisdiction
> > (5) Against whom the victim is protected under the jurisdiction of domestic or family violence laws
>
> **B. Convictions for homicide**, murder, manslaughter, rape, abusive sexual contact, sexual exploitation, incest, torture, trafficking, peonage, holding hostage, involuntary servitude, slave trade, kidnapping, abduction, unlawful criminal restraint, false imprisonment, or an attempt to commit any of these crimes.
>
> **C. At least three convictions for crimes** relating to a controlled substance or alcohol not arising from a single act.

D. Disclosure of criminal history to the beneficiary. If the petition is approved, USCIS will provide a copy of the petition, including the information submitted regarding any protection or restraining orders or criminal history to the Department of State (DOS) for distribution to the beneficiary of the petitioner. USCIS will also provide DOS any criminal background information discovered independently while adjudicating this petition for disclosure to the beneficiary.

NOTE: The name and contact information of any person who was granted a protection or restraining order against you, or of any victim of a crime of violence the petitioner perpetrated, will remain confidential. However, DOS will disclose your relationship to this person or victim (for example, spouse, parent, former spouse) to the beneficiary.

If the petitioner has provided information about a conviction for a crime listed in the I-129F, the USCIS wants to know if they were being battered or subjected to extreme cruelty at the time of conviction. They also want to know if the petitioner:

- Acted in self-defense
- Violated a protection order
- Were convicted of a crime that did not result in serious bodily injury and there was a connection between the crime and petitioner having been battered or subjected to extreme cruelty

The petitioner must also indicate whether they have ever been arrested, cited, charged, indicted, convicted, fined, or imprisoned for breaking or violating any law or ordinance in any country, for any offenses other than those you have already outlined in the previous section. Unless a traffic incident was alcohol- or drug-related or involved a fine of $500 or more, they do not need to provide information on it.

Criminal History Documents

If the petitioner indicated "Yes" to being arrested, cited, charged, indicted, convicted, fined, or imprisoned for breaking or violating any law or ordinance in any country, provide information that explains the circumstances, places, dates, and outcomes for each incident of arrest, citation, charge, indictment, conviction, fine, or imprisonment. You must submit court certified copies of the arrest record and/or disposition for each incident unless you submit a certified statement from the court indicating that no record exists of your arrest, citation, charge, indictment, conviction, fine, or imprisonment.

Multiple I-129F Filers Waiver Request (Not applicable to first-time filers)

The U.S. petitioner must request a waiver for filing multiple I-129F if:

1. The U.S. petitioner is filing this petition on behalf of the foreign fiancé(e) and they have previously filed Form I-129F on behalf of two or more fiancé(e) beneficiaries;

2. The U.S. petitioner is filing this petition on behalf of the foreign fiancé(e) and they have previously had a Form I-129F approved, and less than two years have passed since the filing date of your previously approved petition.

The need for multiple filer waivers comes from the International Marriage Broker Regulation Act (IMBRA) filing limitations.

Select the box that indicates the waiver the U.S. petitioner is requesting. The U.S. petitioner may request and support the waiver with additional information and/or explanation in "Additional Information" or attach a separate sheet of paper. On the separate sheet of paper type or print the petitioner's name and A-Number (if any) at the top of each sheet, indicate the Page Number and Item Number to which the answer refers, and sign and date each sheet.

Types of Waivers (for multiple filers):

General Waiver (multiple filers, No Disqualifying convictions). If the petitioner has never been convicted of a violent criminal offense against a person or persons, submit evidence to show why a waiver is appropriate in the petitioner's case.

Extraordinary Circumstances Waiver (Multiple filers, Prior Convictions for Specified Offenses). If the petitioner has ever been convicted of a violent criminal offense against a person or persons, USCIS will not grant a filing limitations waiver unless the petitioner submits evidence to demonstrate that extraordinary circumstances exist. In addition to evidence explaining the reasons for multiple filings, they must also submit evidence of extraordinary circumstances. Examples of such evidence may include, but are not limited to:

- police reports
- court records
- news articles
- trial transcripts reflecting the nature and circumstances surrounding violent criminal offenses
- rehabilitation
- ties to the community
- records demonstrating good conduct and exemplary service in the uniformed services

Mandatory Waiver (Multiple filers, Prior Criminal Convictions Resulting from **Domestic Violence**). If the petitioner committed violent criminal offenses against a person or persons but were battered or subjected to extreme cruelty by a family member or intimate partner at the time they committed the violent offenses, and they were not the primary perpetrator of violence in the relationship, they may still be eligible for a waiver if USCIS determines that they violated a protection order intended for their protection; they were acting in self-defense; or they committed, were arrested for, were convicted of, or pleaded guilty to committing a crime that did not result in serious bodily injury and there was a connection between the crime committed and them being battered or subjected to extreme cruelty. They must submit evidence explaining the reasons for multiple filings, as well as evidence to support a finding that they qualify for a mandatory waiver based on being subjected to battery or extreme cruelty.

Examples of such evidence may include, but are not limited to:

- police reports
- court records
- news articles
- trial transcripts
- evidence the petitioner acted in self-defense
- evidence the petitioner was a victim of abuse or battery
- the evidence they violated a protection order intended for their protection
- credible evidence that is relevant to their request for a waiver

USCIS cannot approve the petition unless a waiver of the multiple-filing limitation is granted.

Part 4. Biographic Information

In Part 4, the U.S. petitioner provides their biographic information as part of the petition.

Categories and Definitions for Ethnicity and Race. The biographical information asks how the petitioner identifies themselves racially and ethnically.

Height. Select the values that best match the petitioner's height in feet and inches. For example, if the petitioner is five feet and nine inches, select "5" for feet and "09" for inches. Do not enter the height in meters or centimeters.

Weight. Enter the petitioner's weight in pounds. If the petitioner does not know their weight or needs to enter a weight under 30 pounds or over 699 pounds, enter "000." Do not enter the weight in kilograms.

Eye Color. Select the box that best describes the color of the petitioner's eyes.

Hair Color. Select the box that best describes the color of the petitioner's hair or lack of hair.

NOTE: In rare cases, the USCIS may require that the petitioner appear for an interview or provide fingerprints, photograph, and/or signature to verify their identity, obtain additional information, and conduct background and security checks, including a check of criminal history records maintained by the Federal Bureau of Investigation (FBI), before making a decision on the application, petition, or request.

Passport Style Photos

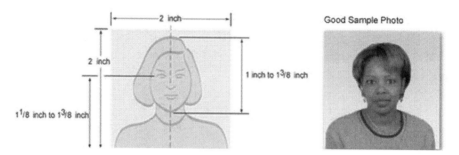

Figure, Passport Style Photo

The I-129F requires a passport style photo from both petitioner and foreign fiancé(e) taken within 30 days of filing this petition. The photos must have a white to off-white background, be printed on thin paper with a glossy finish, and be unmounted and unretouched. The color passport-style photos must be 2 by 2 inches. The photos must be in color with full face, frontal view on a white to off-white background. Head height should measure 1 to 1 3/8 inches from top of hair to bottom of the chin, and eye height is between 1 1/8 to 1 3/8 inches from the bottom of the photo. Your head must be bare unless you are wearing headwear as required by a religious denomination of which you are a member. *Using a pencil or felt pen, lightly print the names of the beneficiary and petitioner and A-Number (if any) on the back of the respective photo.*

Part 5. Petitioner's Statement, Declaration, and Signature

Select the appropriate box to indicate whether the U.S. citizen read this petition themselves or had an interpreter to assist them. If someone assisted the petitioner in completing the petition, select the box indicating that a preparer was used. Further, the petitioner must sign and date their petition and provide the daytime telephone number, mobile telephone number (if any), and email address (if any). Every petition MUST contain the signature of the petitioner (or parent or legal guardian, if applicable). *A stamped or typewritten name in place of a signature is not acceptable.*

Part 6. Interpreter's Contact Information, Certification, and Signature

If the petitioner uses anyone as an interpreter to read the instructions and questions on this petition to the petitioner in a language in which they are fluent, the interpreter must fill out this section, provide his or her name, the name and address of his or her business or organization (if any), his or her daytime telephone number, his or her mobile telephone number (if any), and his or her email address (if any). The interpreter must sign and date the petition.

Part 7. Contact Information, Declaration, and Signature of the Person Preparing this Petition, if Other Than the Petitioner

This section must contain the signature of the person who completed the petition, if other than the petitioner. If the same individual acted as an interpreter and a preparer, that person should complete both Part 6. and Part 7. If the person who completed this petition is associated with a business or organization, that person should complete the business or organization name and address information. Anyone who helped the petitioner complete this petition MUST sign and date the petition. A stamped or typewritten name in place of a signature is not acceptable. If the person who helped the petitioner prepare the petition is an attorney or accredited representative whose representation extends beyond preparation of this petition, he or she may be obliged to also submit a completed Form G-28, Notice of Entry of Appearance as Attorney or Accredited Representative, or Form G-28I, Notice of Entry of Appearance as Attorney in Matters Outside the Geographical Confines of the United States, along with the petition.

Part 8. Additional Information

If the petitioner needs extra space to provide any additional information within this petition, use the space provided in "Additional Information" or attach a separate sheet of paper. On the separate sheet of paper type or print the petitioner's name and A-Number (if any) at the top of each sheet, indicate the Page Number and Item Number to which the answer refers, and sign and date each sheet.

Step 1.2 - Declaration of How We Met

The U.S. petitioner needs to create a document that explains how they met the foreign fiancé(e). They must indicate in Part 2 of the I-129F that they met in person and provide evidence of meeting in person. A declaration of how you met is a written statement from the petitioner stating the circumstances of the meeting. The declaration should mention both names, how, where and when the couple met. The time frame of the meeting must be within two years of filing the I-129F. The U.S. petitioner should also sign the document.

Figure, Declaration of How We Met, Form I-129F

Bruce Brown
1122 Pikes Creek
Takoma, Seattle WA 98105
(206)734-0962
bruce.brown@gmail.com

United States Department of Homeland Security
U.S. Citizenship and Immigration Services
Attn: I-129F
2501 South State Highway 121 Business
Suite 400
Lewisville, TX 75067

25 April 2014

Subject: Declaration of How We Met, Form I-129F

To Whom It May Concern:

This declaration expands on Form I-129F. The purpose is to describe the circumstances under which Yuri Sincero and I, Bruce Brown, met.

We met in 2011 online. We began as friends but overtime we became more. I traveled to Cebu to meet her in June 2012 and we realized we had such a close bond that we wanted to become serious. We have met every time we could since 2012. Which is on average about every 5 months. We have lived together up to 1 month. We have met in part of the Philippines, Indonesia and Singapore as well.

We have talked to each other everyday since we met in 2011 and literally have only miss days if there is a catastrophic disaster such as flood, earthquake, or typhoon when it was impossible to talk.

Signed,

Bruce Brown

Step 1.3 - Proof of Meeting

Evidence of this meeting may include, but is not limited to, a written statement from the petitioner and/or the foreign fiancé(e) stating the circumstances of their meeting (see "declaration of how we met" & "Supporting Evidence of Meeting" for an example). If you believe you qualify for an exception to the in-person meeting requirement, submit evidence that supports the exception (for more information see the section called: *"2 Year Meeting Requirement Waiver and Exception"*).

A supporting declaration document that explains all the evidence will help the USCIS have a comprehensive view of your relationship.

NOTE: The examples displayed in this book are not the only documents you can use to show proof of meeting. There are other kinds of documents you can use, but what is most important is that you have the names, date, and location displayed on the documents to show evidence of the petitioner and foreign fiancé(e) meeting within the last two years before filing. Pictures are also important, but pictures alone may not be enough.

Figure, Support Evidence of Meeting

Subject: I-129F Supporting Evidence of Meeting/Co-habitation within 2 years (prior to filing)

To Whom It May Concern:

This is an addendum to the I-129F to show that Yuri Sincero (alien fiance) and Bruce (petitioner), met and/or lived together during the following time periods:

Time Period	Location	Notes/supporting documents
May 12, 2012 - End of May 2012	Cebu City, Boracay (Philippines)	Marriott Cebu City receipt, Cebu Pacific ticket Cebu - Boracay
Aug 15, 2012 - 7 Sept 2012	Philippines & Thailand	Reservations, Airline tickets, train tickets
Feb 01, 2013 - 18 Feb 2013	Pattaya, Thailand	Reservations, airline tickets
May 25, 2013 - 3 June 2013	Hong Kong	Hotel Reservations, Airline tickets Passport Visa
Aug 2013 - Sept 2013 *(lived together)*	Cebu City, Philippines	Airline tickets
April 21, 2014 - *pending approx. 30 days*	Pattaya, Thailand	Pre-purchased tickets, itinerary, receipt SIAM House deposit

Copies of documents submitted are exact photocopies of unaltered documents and I understand that I may be required to submit original documents to an Immigration or Consular officer at a later date.

Explanation of Supporting Evidence of Meeting

Item Number (1) of the supporting evidence (Figure, Support Evidence of Meeting) is a hotel receipt (*Figure, Hotel Receipt*) added to the I-129F package. The receipt places the U.S. petitioner (Bruce Brown) to the location (Cebu, Philippines) within two years of filing. Since the date of this receipt is 2012, the U.S. petitioner would have to file by 2014.

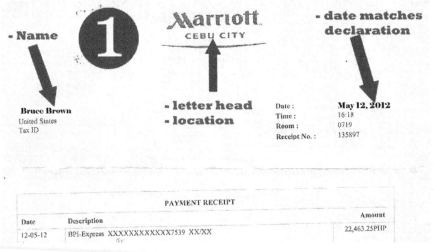

Figure, Hotel Receipt

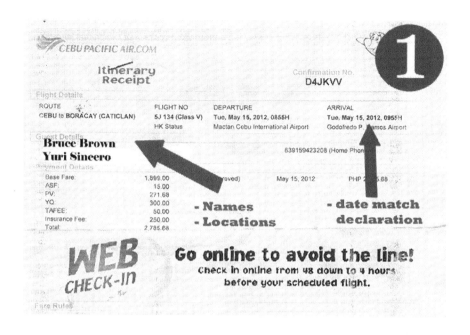

Figure, An itinerary receipt

Item Number (1) of the supporting evidence (Figure, Support Evidence of Meeting) mentions an airline itinerary (Figure, an Itinerary receipt) added to the I-129F package (this can be a copy or original receipt). The receipt places the U.S. petitioner (Bruce Brown) & beneficiary (Yuri Sincero) on the same flight (from Cebu to Boracay, Philippines). The date of the receipt is within two years of filing. Since the date of this receipt is 2012, the U.S. petitioner would have to file by 2014.

53

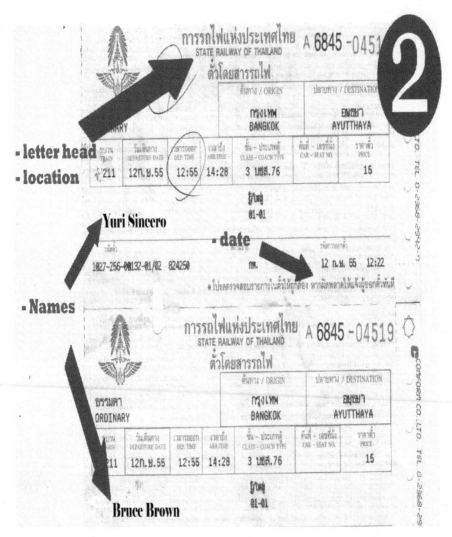

Figure, Train Receipt

Item Number (2) of the supporting evidence (Figure, Support Evidence of Meeting) is a train receipt in Thailand. The names of both fiancé(e)s are on the receipt. The location and date are on the receipt.

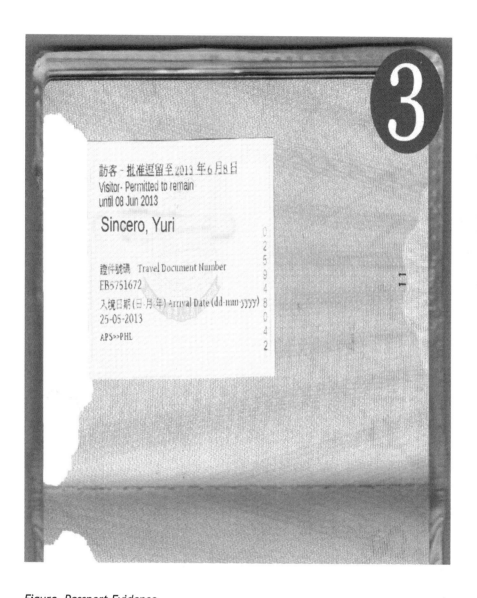

Figure, Passport Evidence

Item Number (3) of the supporting evidence (Figure, Support Evidence of Meeting) is a copy of a Hong Kong visa in the beneficiary's passport.

Figure, Boarding Passes with Names, Date, Locations

The boarding pass evidence has the names of the couple, dates that are within the two years of filing, and locations showing evidence that the two were together.

Figure, Airline Booking with Names, Date, and Location

The flight confirmation page shows the names of the U.S. petitioner and the foreign fiancé(e) in passenger details. The booking date shows a meeting occurring within two years of filing the I-129F (2014). It also has locations that match up with other evidence.

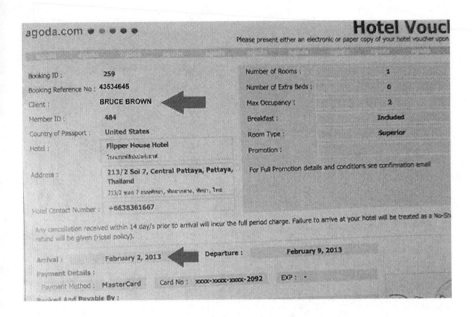

Figure, Hotel Booking with Names, Dates, and Location

Notice that the Arrival and Departure date of the hotel booking is within two years of us filing the I-129f. We filed in 2014. This helps to establish a meeting in person within two years of filing.

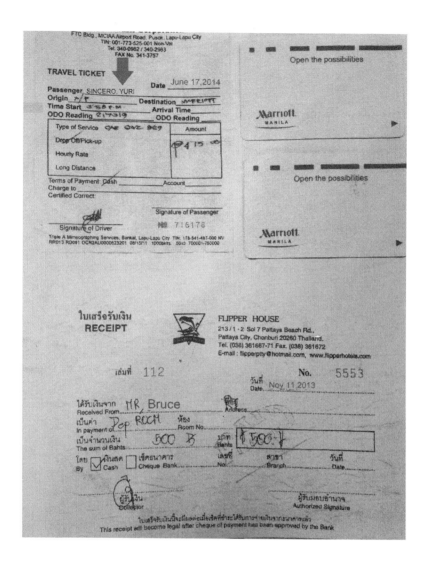

Figure, Travel Ticket & Hotel Receipt

The most effective evidence from receipts and tickets will display the name, locations and time.

Figure, Cebu Air Tickets and Lyric Hotel Management in Cebu

These tickets and receipts show the name of the petitioner and the location and date. This gives more evidence that the petitioner was in that location

Include Pictures as Evidence of Meeting in Person

Include a few pictures that show that the petitioner and the foreign fiancé(e) met physically in person. The best pictures look recent, clearly show faces and landmarks of the places that the couple have been together. Use itineraries, tickets, and receipts that complement the pictures of the couple. For example, if there are receipts of being in Thailand together, show pictures of Thailand in the background of the pictures.

Figure, Picture in Hong Kong

Figure, Picture in Thailand

Figure, Picture together with Thailand in the background

Figure, Picture in Cebu Philippines

Use of Copies

Submit copies of all receipts instead of the original (unless the USCIS or Department of State asks for the original). You may need the original for additional copies. Just make sure the photocopies you submit are legible.

2 Year Meeting Requirement Waiver and Exception

The I-129F mentions exceptions for the two-year meeting requirement. These exceptions include:

> (1) The requirement for the U.S. petitioner to meet the fiancé(e) in person would violate strict and long-established customs of the fiancé(e)'s culture or social practice, and that any and all aspects of the traditional arrangements have been or will be met in accordance with the custom or practice.

> (2) The requirement for the U.S. petitioner to meet the fiancé(e) in person would result in extreme hardship to the petitioner.

NOTE: Although the I-129F clearly states that this is possible, we have not seen this work for anyone. The meeting requirement is strictly enforced. Approval with an exception letter and evidence seems possible, but highly improbable.

Step 1.4 - Letter of Intent to Marry - Petitioner & Beneficiary

Create a single letter signed by both the U.S. petitioner and the foreign fiancé(e) (or two separate letters signed by each) that explains their intent to marry within 90-days of the foreign fiancé(e) getting to the USA. *Make sure they are both signed!*

Dear Sir or Madam:

I, Bruce Brown, do hereby state that I am legally able and willing to marry Yuri Sincero. I intend to do so within 90 days of her arrival to the US using the K-1 visa.

Being away from her has caused me great heartache. I am ready to start a new life with her. She makes me very happy. I am very blessed to have found such an amazing match. I am honored that she would have me as her husband.

Yours truly,

Brukjlk Bekn
Bruce Brown

Figure, Intent to Marry - U.S. petitioner

Yuri Sincero
#18 Manga St Opra Blvd
Cebu City, Philippines 6000
pinalove24@gmail.com

United States Department of Homeland Security
U.S. Citizenship and Immigration Services
Attn: I-129F
2501 South State Highway 121 Business
Suite 400
Lewisville, TX 75067

25 April 2014

Dear Sir or Madam:

I, Yuri M. Sincero, do hereby state that I am legally able and willing to marry Bruce Brown. I intend to do so within 90 days of my arrival to the US using the K-1 visa.

Being away from the man that I really love has been very hard and lonely. I have been ready to start a joyous home with him. His love has given me contentment and satisfaction in life beyond material things. I am very thankful that I found my match. I am very proud of having a great man and I am so honored that he would have me as his wife.

Yours truly,

yuriS

Yuri Sincero

Figure, Intent to Marry - Foreign Fiancé(e)

Step 1.5 - If Applicable Essential - Divorce, Birth Certificate

In this section, we cover supporting evidence that is essential to proving that the U.S. petitioner and foreign fiancé(e) are eligible to apply for the K-1 fiancé(e) visa. Some of these may not be applicable to every situation. For example, if the petitioner or foreign fiancé(e) have never been married, they will **not** have to provide a divorce or annulment document.

Birth Certificate/Naturalization Documents

If the petitioner was born in the USA, include a copy of the petitioner's U.S. birth certificate or naturalization documents as evidence that they are eligible to apply for a petition for the foreign fiancé(e). This does not need to be an original or notarized copy, a photocopy is fine, but make sure it is clear so the USCIS can read it.

Figure, Birth Certificate

Eligible to Marry: Divorce, Annulment, Widow

If the U.S. petitioner or the foreign fiancé(e) have ever been married in the past, they must include a copy of the original divorce decree, annulment or death certificate. These documents must be provided for ALL previous marriages. It does not matter how long ago the marriages were. In the US, you can usually find previous divorce/ annulment/death certificate records at the local county where the event occurred. If a previous spouse passed away, the petitioner or foreign fiancé(e) must have a death certificate.

SUPERIOR COURT OF THE STATE OF CALIFORNIA
FOR THE COUNTY OF LOS ANGELES

COUNTY OF ORANGE
Plaintiff,
vs.
COUNTY OF LOS ANGELES
Defendant.

FINAL JUDGMENT OF DIVORCE

In this cause an interlocutory judgment was entered on the ......**11TH**.............. day of **MARCH**............**1889**......, adjudging that plaintiff was entitled to a divorce from defendant, and more than one year having elapsed, and no appeal having been taken from said judgment, and no motion for a new trial having been granted and the action not having been dismissed;

Court's
Now, upon the plaintiff's motion, it is adjudged that plaintiff be and is granted a final defendant's judgment of divorce from defendant and that the bonds of matrimony between plaintiff and defendant be, and the same are, dissolved.

It is further ordered and adjudged that wherein said interlocutory judgment makes any provision for alimony or the custody and support of children, said provision be and the same is hereby made binding on the parties affected thereby the same as if herein set forth in full, and that wherein said interlocutory judgment relates to the property of the parties hereto, said property be and the same is hereby assigned in accordance with the terms thereof to the parties therein declared to be entitled thereto, and wherein said interlocutory judgment makes provision for restoration of the maiden name of the wife or the name under which she was married, the said maiden name of the wife or the name under which she was married is hereby restored as in said interlocutory judgment provided.

Dated **March 11, 1964**..............................

Figure, Divorce Decree Sample

Evidence of Legal Name Change

If the U.S. petitioner or foreign fiancé(e) has ever legally changed their names, they need to indicate those names in the I-129F Part 1 and 2 "other names" used and provide evidence of any other official names. This is necessary if the U.S. petitioner or beneficiary have had an official name change but might also be on an adoption decree, marriage certificate, or court order.

Figure, Evidence of Legal Name Change

Step 1.6 - Optional Forms - G-1145 & Cover Letter

The cover letter and G-1145 are optional forms. The cover letter acts as a table of contents for the entire package and G-1145 is an E-Notification of Application/Petition Acceptance.

Cover Letter

The cover letter is a document you create that lists all the items inside the I-129F package (including the fee and the I-129F form itself). It is placed on top of all the documents. The cover letter makes it easier for the USCIS to find each of the required documents in the package.

Bruce Brown
11200 Pikes Creek
Seattle, WA 11117

United States Department of Homeland Security
U.S. Citizenship and Immigration Services
Attn: I-129F
2501 South State Highway 121 Business
Suite 400
Lewisville, TX 75067

16 April 2014

Nature of the submission: Form I-129F, Petition for K-1 Fiancé

To Whom It May Concern:

Enclosed please find my Form I-129F, Petition for K-1 Fiancé Visa for Yuri Sincero, and supporting documents.

Contents include:
- Money Order payment in the amount of [$XXX.XX].
- I-129F
- I-129F Supplement: Declaration of How We Met in person
- Passport style photo (Petitioner)
- Passport style photo (Beneficiary)
- Birth certificate (Petitioner)
- Divorce Decree
- Letter certifying intent to marry (Petitioner and Beneficiary)
- Proof of having met in person in the past two years

Copies of documents submitted are exact photocopies of unaltered documents and I understand that I may be required to submit original documents to an Immigration or Consular officer at a later date.

Signed,

Bruce Brown

Figure, Cover Letter

G-1145 E-Notification

Filling out the G-1145, E-Notification of Application/Petition Acceptance allows the USCIS to send an email or text to the contact information provided when they receive the package. They will send the receipt number and tell the petitioner how to get case status information.

e-Notification of Application/Petition Acceptance
Department of Homeland Security
U.S. Citizenship and Immigration Services

USCIS
Form G-1145

What Is the Purpose of This Form?

Use this form to request an electronic notification (e-Notification) when U.S. Citizenship and Immigration Services accepts your immigration application. This service is available for applications filed at a USCIS Lockbox facility.

General Information

Complete the information below and clip this form to the first page of your application package. You will receive one e-mail and/or text message for each form you are filing.

We will send the e-Notification within 24 hours after we accept your application. Domestic customers will receive an e-mail and/or text message; overseas customers will only receive an e-mail. Undeliverable e-Notifications cannot be resent.

The e-mail or text message will display your receipt number and tell you how to get updated case status information. It will not include any personal information. The e-Notification does not grant any type of status or benefit; rather it is provided as a convenience to customers.

USCIS will also mail you a receipt notice (I-797C), which you will receive within 10 days after your application has been accepted; use this notice as proof of your pending application or petition.

USCIS Privacy Act Statement

AUTHORITIES: The information requested on this form is collected pursuant to section 103(a) of the Immigration and Nationality Act, as amended INA section 101, et seq.

PURPOSE: The primary purpose for providing the information on this form is to request an electronic notification when USCIS accepts immigration form. The information you provide will be used to send you a text and/or email message.

DISCLOSURE: The information you provide is voluntary. However, failure to provide the requested information may prevent USCIS from providing you a text and/or email message receipting your immigration form.

ROUTINE USES: The information provided on this form will be used by and disclosed to DHS personnel and contractors in accordance with approved routine uses, as described in the associated published system of records notices [DHS/USCIS-007-Benefit Information System and DHS/USCIS-001 - Alien File (A-File) and Central Index System (CIS), which can be found at www.dhs.gov/privacy]. The information may also be made available, as appropriate for law enforcement purposes or in the interest of national security.

Complete this form and clip it on top of the first page of your immigration form(s).		
Applicant/Petitioner Full Last Name	Applicant/Petitioner Full First Name	Applicant/Petitioner Full Middle Name
Email Address		Mobile Phone Number (Text Message)

Figure, G-1145, e-Notification of Application / Petition Acceptance

Step 1.7 - Submit Package & Payment

Once the petitioner has the Form I-129F and the supporting evidence, they will send it all together to the USCIS as one package.

Figure, Package Submission

The filing fee for the I-129F is $535USD. Always double check this and other fees listed since they change often (filing fee: https://www.uscis.gov/i-129f). The U.S. petitioner can pay the K-1 fiancé(e) filing fee by money order, personal check, cashier's check, or credit card.

Form G-1450, Authorization for Credit Card Transaction is used to pay with a credit card (Access the credit card transaction form here: https://www.uscis.gov/g-1450).

Authorization for Credit Card Transactions

Department of Homeland Security
U.S. Citizenship and Immigration Services

USCIS
Form G-1450
OMB No. 1615-0131
Expires 01/31/2021

How To Fill Out Form G-1450

1. Type or print legibly in black ink.

2. Complete the "Applicant's/Petitioner's/Requester's Information," "Credit Card Billing Information," and "Credit Card Information" sections and sign the authorization.

3. Place your Form G-1450 ON TOP of your application, petition, or request package.

NOTE: Failure to provide the requested information may result in USCIS and your financial institution not accepting the payment. USCIS cannot process credit card payments without an authorized signature.

NOTE: Form G-1450 may only be used with a form being submitted to a USCIS Lockbox. **Do not submit this form to a USCIS Field Office. They will not accept it.**

> We recommend that you print or save a copy of your completed Form G-1450 to review in the future and for your records.

Applicant's/Petitioner's/Requester's Information (Full Legal Name)

Given Name (First Name)	Middle Name (if any)	Family Name (Last Name)

Credit Card Billing Information (Credit Card Holder's Name as it Appears on the Card)

Given Name (First Name)	Middle Name (if any)	Family Name (Last Name)

Credit Card Holder's Billing Address:

Street Number and Name	Apt. Ste. Flr. ☐ ☐ ☐	Number
City or Town	State	ZIP Code

Credit Card Holder's Signature and Contact Information:

Credit Card Holder's Signature
Credit Card Holder's Daytime Telephone Number	Credit Card Holder's Email Address

Credit Card Information

Credit Card Number	Credit Card Type:	☐ Visa ☐ MasterCard ☐ American Express ☐ Discover	Authorized Payment Amount $ .00
Credit Card Expiration Date (mm/yyyy)			

Figure, Authorization for Credit Card Transaction

#YuriBruce: Visa Approved series

Package Submission Address

File Form I-129F at the USCIS Dallas Lockbox facility:
For U.S. Postal Service (USPS):
>USCIS
>P.O. Box 660151
>Dallas, TX 75266

For FedEx, UPS, and DHL deliveries:
>USCIS
>Attn: I-129F
>2501 South State Highway 121 Business
>Suite 400
>Lewisville, TX 75067

Filing Tips for Form I-129F
Complete all sections of the form. USCIS will reject the form if these fields are missing:

- Part 1. Information About the petitioner
  - Classification Sought for the Beneficiary
  - Family Name
  - Petitioner's Mailing Address
  - Date of Birth
- Part 2. Information About the Beneficiary
  - Classification Sought for Beneficiary
  - Family Name
  - Date of Birth

The petitioners must sign the form! USCIS will reject and return any unsigned form.

Step 1. References:

"I-129F, Petition for Alien Fiancé(e)."   USCIS, 5 May 2018, https://www.uscis.gov/i-129f
"Visas for Fiancé(e)s of U.S. Citizens." USCIS, 5 May 2018, https://www.uscis.gov/family/family-us-citizens/visas-fiancees-us-citizens
"Form I-129F Instructions." USCIS, 5 May 2018, https://www.uscis.gov/sites/default/files/files/form/i-129finstr.pdf
"G-1145, E-Notification of Application/Petition Acceptance." USCIS, 5 May 2018, https://www.uscis.gov/g-1145
"Form I-797: Types and Functions."   USCIS, 5 May 2018, https://www.uscis.gov/i-797-info

Step 2. National Visa Center

Step 2.0 - National Visa Center (NVC) Overview

Welcome to Step 2 of Fiancé(e) Visa to USA! In this step, we will talk about what happens after the petitioner submits the I-129F Package. We will explain what an "NOA" and an "RFE" are. We will also show how to check the status of the case and what the foreign fiancé(e) should be doing while waiting for the I-129F to be approved.

National Visa Center Checklist

National Visa Center Checklist	
Tasks/Documents	
Get Confirmation of USCIS Decision. If the USCIS decision is "APPROVED", the U.S. petitioner or foreign fiancé(e) needs to contact the National Visa Center to get the case number. If the USCIS is other than approved, then the U.S. petitioner needs to read the instructions on the documents sent by the USCIS.	
Contact the National Visa Center. The National Visa Center will send mail to the U.S. petitioner about receiving the approved I-129F package with the visa case number and instructions on what to do next. The U.S. petitioner can also call or email the National Visa Center to get the case number.	
Use the Case Number to Track the Visa Status. With the visa case number, the U.S. petitioner can track visa status at https://ceac.state.gov/ceac/	
Embassy Preparation. Once approved, the foreign fiancé(e) should start Step 3.	
Other Approved / Request for More Evidence. In some cases, the I-129F package is rejected or requires more evidence. In these cases, the USCIS will state why the request was rejected or give instructions on what they need from the U.S. petitioner. **Comply as soon as possible.**	

Figure, U.S. Department of State National Visa Center

Before we dive in, let's talk about the National Visa Center. The USCIS forwards the approved I-129F petition to the National Visa Center (NVC) in Portsmouth, New Hampshire for visa pre-processing. NVC is under the Department of State.

Figure, USCIS to NVC to Embassy

The Department of State is a different department of government than the USCIS. USCIS is *"U.S. Citizenship and Immigration Services administers the nation's lawful immigration system, safeguarding its integrity and promise by efficiently and fairly adjudicating requests for immigration benefits while protecting Americans, securing the homeland, and honoring our values."* The U.S. Department of State is the U.S. federal executive department that advises the President and represents the country in international affairs and foreign policy issues. During the K-1 visa process, the USCIS processes the I-129F and the green card, while the Department of State creates K-1 visa (if approved). The USCIS and Department of State work together to make sure the foreign national, the U.S. petitioner, and the USA are safe.

The NVC pre-process many other visas. For K-1 visas, they forward the I-129F package to the U.S. embassy mentioned on the I-129F.

Step 2.1 - I-797 Notice of Action

After submission of the I-129F, the petitioner will receive (3) letters from the U.S. government. (2) letters are called "notice of actions", Form I-797 from the USCIS and (1) letter is from the U.S. State Department, National Visa Center, once the package gets approved.

Notice of Action Receipt (NOA 1)

Notice of Action #1 (Figure, Notice of Action Receipt) - NOA1 is from the USCIS, this is a receipt of payment. This is to inform the petitioner that USCIS has received the package and the payment. Getting the receipt takes between 2 - 4 weeks after submission but can take longer if the USCIS is backlogged with packages. With the first notice of action, you can use the receipt number to check the status of your I-129F package (USCIS.gov).

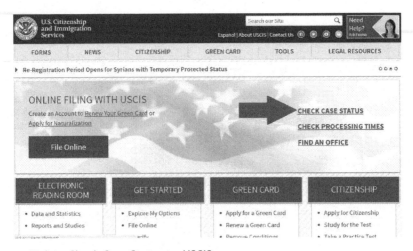

Figure, Link to Check Case Status on USCIS

Department of Homeland Security U.S. Citizenship and Immigration Services	Form I-797C, Notice of Action

THIS NOTICE DOES NOT GRANT ANY IMMIGRATION STATUS OR BENEFIT.

NOTICE TYPE Receipt	NOTICE DATE April 24, 2014
CASE TYPE I-129F, Petition for Alien Fiance(e)	USCIS ALIEN NUMBER
RECEIPT NUMBER WCC1494412244	RECEIVED DATE April 24, 2014	PAGE 1 of 1
		DATE OF BIRTH December 24, 1974

BRUCE B. BROWN
C/O BRUCE B. BROWN
1122 PIKES CREEK
TAKOMA, SEATTLE WA 90205

PAYMENT INFORMATION:	
Application/Petition Fee:	$340.00
Biometrics Fee:	$0.00
Total Amount Received:	$340.00
Total Balance Due:	$0.00

APPLICANT/PETITIONER NAME AND MAILING ADDRESS

The I-129F, Petition for Alien Fiance(e) has been received by our office for the following beneficiaries and is in process:

Name SINCERO, YURI M.	Date of Birth 11/11/1986	Country of Birth PHILIPPINES	Class (If Applicable)

Please verify your personal information listed above and immediately notify the USCIS National Customer Service Center at the phone number listed below if there are any changes.

Please note that if a priority date is printed on this notice, the priority does not reflect earlier retained priority dates.

If you have questions about possible immigration benefits and services, filing information, or USCIS forms, please call the USCIS National Customer Service Center (NCSC) at **1-800-375-5283**. If you are hearing impaired, please call the NCSC TDD at **1-800-767-1833**. Please also refer to the USCIS website: www.uscis.gov.

If you have any questions or comments regarding this notice or the status of your case, please contact our customer service number.

You will be notified separately about any other case you may have filed.

Figure, Notice of Action Receipt

Notice of Action Approval (NOA 2)

Notice of Action #2 (Figure, Notice of Action Approval) - The NOA2 is issued from the USCIS when the petition is approved. It will tell the petitioner what is going to happen next.

How long it takes to get the notice of action approval depends on the USCIS staff. If they have a high number of packages, it can take longer. It also depends on your case. We have seen it take between 45 days - 8 months. It can be the longest or shortest part of the process. The length of time depends on how busy the USCIS is and how long it takes them to examine the I-129F package.

Once the petitioner gets the NOA2, they need to contact the National Visa Center and get the case number. The case number is attached to the package before it is sent to the U.S. embassy near the foreign fiancé(e).

Contact the National Visa Center at (603) 334-0700
　　　　　Email: NVCINQUIRY@state.gov
It takes the NVC about 7 - 14 days to create the case number.

Department of Homeland Security
U.S. Citizenship and Immigration Services

I-797, Notice of Action

THE UNITED STATES OF AMERICA

RECEIPT NUMBER WCC-11-224-44444		CASE TYPE I129F PETITION FOR FIANCE(E)
RECEIPT DATE April 28, 2014	PRIORITY DATE	PETITIONER BROWN, BRUCE B.
NOTICE DATE May 24, 2014	PAGE 1 of 1	BENEFICIARY A222 444 111 SINCERO, YURI M.

BRUCE BROWN
C/O BRUCE BROWN
1122 Pikes Creek
Takoma, Seattle WA 90205

Notice Type: Approval Notice
Valid from 05/24/2014 to 09/22/2014

The above petition has been approved. We have sent the original visa petition to the Department of State National Visa Center (NVC), 32 Rochester Avenue, Portsmouth, NH 03801-2909. The USCIS has completed all action; further inquiries should be directed to the NVC.

The NVC now processes all approved fiance(e) petitions. The NVC processing should be complete within two to four weeks after receiving the petition from USCIS. The NVC will create a case record with your petition information. NVC will then send the petition to the U.S. Embassy or Consulate where your fiance(e) will be interviewed for his or her visa.

You will receive notification by mail when NVC has sent your petition to the U.S. Embassy or Consulate. The notification letter will provide you with a unique number for your case and the name and address of the U.S. Embassy or Consulate where your petition has been sent.

You should allow a minimum of 30 days for Department of State processing before contacting the NVC. If you have not received any correspondence from the NVC within 30 days, you may contact the NVC by e-mail at NVCINQUIRY@state.gov. You will need to enter the USCIS receipt number from this approval notice in the subject line. In order to receive information about your petition, you will need to include the Petitioner's name and date of birth, and the Applicant's name and date of birth, in the body of the e-mail.

THIS FORM IS NOT A VISA AND MAY NOT BE USED IN PLACE OF A VISA.

When the person this petition is for enters the U.S. based on this visa, he or she will be admitted for ninety (90) days in order to marry the petitioner, and based on that marriage file for adjustment to permanent resident status on Form I-485. The form to apply for adjustment can be obtained at any local USCIS office or USCIS forms center. Please attach a copy of this notice to the adjustment application when you file it.

If the petitioner and the fiance(e) do not marry within these 90 days, status will expire, and he or she will be in violation of the Immigration and Nationality Act if he or she does not depart. An extension cannot be granted. It is requested that the petitioner inform his or her local USCIS office if he or she determines that the marriage will not take place within the 90 day period. Please attach a copy of this notice to any correspondence about this case.

NOTICE: Although this application/petition has been approved, USCIS and the U.S. Department of Homeland Security reserve the right to verify the information submitted in this application, petition and/or supporting documentation to ensure conformity with applicable laws, rules, regulations, and other authorities. Methods used for verifying information may include, but are not limited to, the review of public and private information sources, the Internet, or telephone, and site inspections of businesses and residences. Information obtained during the course of verification will be used to determine whether revocation, rescission, and/or removal proceedings are appropriate. Applicants, petitioners, and representatives of record will be provided an opportunity to address derogatory information before any formal proceeding is initiated.

Please see the additional information on the back. You will be notified separately about any other cases you filed.
U.S. CITIZENSHIP & IMMIGRATION SVC.
CALIFORNIA SERVICE CENTER
P. O. BOX 30111
LAGUNA NIGUEL   CA   92607-0111
Customer Service Telephone: (800) 375-5283

Form I-797 (Rev. 01/31/05) N

#YuriBruce: Visa Approved series

Figure, Notice of Action Approval

Letter from National Visa Center

The Department of State, NVC letter - This letter is issued when the NVC receives the I-129F package from the USCIS. It will have instructions on what to do next. Once the National Visa Center gets the package, they assign a case number and send it to the proper U.S. embassy (based on information provided in the I-129F). It takes them 10 - 45 days to send it to the U.S. embassy. The petitioner can contact the National Visa Center to get the case number or wait for the letter which has the case number on it.

BRUCE MICHAEL BROWN
1122 PIKES CREEK
SEATTLE, WA 34754

June 20, 2014

Dear BRUCE MICHAEL BROWN :

The National Visa Center (NVC) received your fiancé(e)'s approved I-129F petition from U.S. Citizenship and Immigration Services (USCIS). The NVC will now forward the petition to the U.S. Embassy or Consulate in MANILA. The U.S. Embassy or Consulate will contact your fiancé(e) when they are ready to process his or her petition.

In the meantime, please have your fiancé(e) and his or her children visit ceac.state.gov and complete Form DS-160 to apply for a K visa.

Please keep the following information for your records:

Case Number............................MNL20144784875

USCIS Receipt Number..................WAC5838512234

Principal Applicant......................YURI MAHINAY SINCERO

Petitioner.................................BRUCE MICHAEL BROWN

Interview Location.....................MANILA
U.S. EMBASSY
1201 ROXAS BOULEVARD
MANILA
PHILIPPINES

Sincerely,

U.S. Department of State
Bureau of Consular Affairs

Figure, Letter from National Visa Center

Request for Evidence (RFE)

Let's talk about RFE and Rejections. Not everyone gets approved immediately.

Notice of Action "RFE" - An RFE is a request for more evidence. If the USCIS need more information, they will send a Notice of Action that tells you exactly what they want before they can continue. It is important that you read it very carefully, and don't delay. Returning the requested evidence will have a time limit.

Notice of Action "Rejection" - In some rare cases, the USCIS will send a notice of action that flat out rejects the petition. Reasons for rejections include (but are not limited to) not signing the I-129F, not including the fee, not putting enough evidence, filling out the I-129F wrong. These are just a few reasons that the I-129F can be rejected. In many cases, the USCIS does not even bother to send an NOA rejection. They just send the package back. If you are lucky enough to receive a rejection letter they will explain why the petition was rejected.

If the package is rejected, with no explanation, go through all the instructions in the book and double check everything.

Step 2.2 - Contact National Visa Center (NVC)

After approval of the I-129F package, the petitioner or the foreign fiancé(e) can contact the National Visa Center to get the immigrant visa case number.

Email (immigrant visa inquiries only): NVCINQUIRY@state.gov .
Type the notice of action receipt number or case number in the subject line of the email and ask for the case number or ask for status.

Phone (for immigrant visa inquiries only): (603) 334-0700. Customer Service Representatives can speak with applicants Monday through Friday from 7:00 a.m. to 12:00 midnight EST, excluding holidays.

Phone (for nonimmigrant visa inquiries only): (603) 334-0888. Customer Service Representatives can speak with applicants Monday through Friday from 7:00 a.m. to 12:00 midnight EST, excluding holidays.

When you call, have your receipt number (or case number if that has already been obtained), petitioner's full name, and the beneficiary's full name and date of birth available.

Mail (for immigrant visa inquiries only):
National Visa Center
Attn: WC
31 Rochester Avenue
Suite 200
Portsmouth, NH 03801-2915

Contact the U.S. Embassy

If you know that the NVC has already sent out your package to the U.S. embassy, and want to contact the state department directly, you will have to call the actual U.S. embassy that will be processing the case.

Each embassy has their own website, so you will have to do some research on how to contact them. Here is a list of U.S. embassies:

- https://www.usembassy.gov/

Contact Congress

In some rare cases, the U.S. embassy, USCIS, or even the NVC really messes up or delays your process. Sometimes they lose the package or make the wrong analysis of the package. In this case, the first thing you should do is try to work with them. If they are willing to work with you, then be patient. If they refuse to work with you, the U.S. petitioner may need to get an immigration lawyer or contact their congressperson. Let the U.S. embassy, USCIS, or NVC know that the petitioner is contacting Congress.

- **Contact Congress person:** https://www.house.gov/representatives/find-your-representative.

Believe it or not, the U.S. petitioner's congressperson really can influence the process. It may take longer if the congressperson has to get involved but sometimes it is the only option. Telling the USCIS, NVC, or embassy that the U.S. petitioner is going to call their congress may speed up the process.

Another option to consider is an immigration lawyer. If you do decide to get one, find one with many years of experience that has good reviews. You can find these immigration lawyers online. They are not cheap and cannot guarantee success.

Step 2.3 - Check the Status

If you are in a long-distance relationship, the waiting is really the hardest part of the K-1 visa process. You can check the status of the I-129F package at the USCIS or if your package is already with the National Visa Center, you can check the status of your case number.

To check the status of the I-129F package go to this USCIS.gov site and look for "Check your Status".

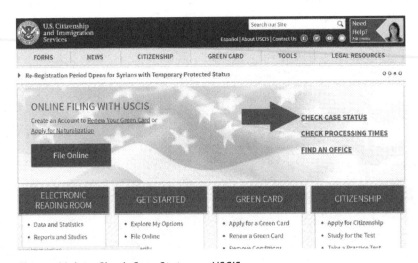

Figure, Link to Check Case Status on USCIS

Use the receipt number on the top of the notice of action approval to check the case status on the USCIS.gov site.

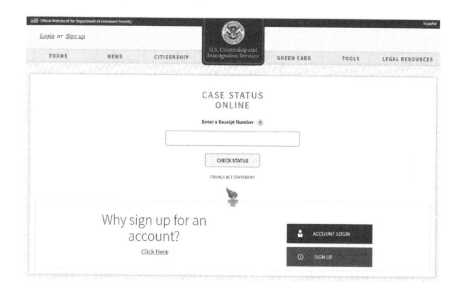

Figure, USCIS Check Status

You can also call them (800-375-5283). The contact information of the USCIS is under "Contact Us" on their site.

Once the package is sent from the NVC to the U.S. embassy, you can check the status of your K-1 visa case with the State Department on the Consular Electronic Application Center (CEAC) https://ceac.state.gov/ceacstattracker/

This requires the Immigrant Visa Case Number from the NVC.

Figure, Visa Status Check (U.S. Department of State)

Step 2.4 - Foreign Fiancé(e) Prepare While Waiting

Up to this point, we have been mostly talking to the U.S. petitioner because, in the beginning, it is mostly them that has to prepare the package for the USCIS.

Pretty soon it will be the foreign fiancé(e) that has to prepare for the interview with the U.S. State Department at the U.S. embassy. While waiting for the I-129F to be approved and the National Visa Center to send the package to the U.S. embassy, there are things that the foreign fiancé(e) can do to start getting ready:

- Make sure their passport is not going to expire within 6 months of getting a U.S. visa
- If they don't have a passport, get one
- Police Clearance (in their own country and places they worked abroad)
- Gather important documents (birth certificate, school records, divorce/annulment)
- Gather Armed services records
- Get a passport style photo
- Save money for medical exam, travel, and making copies
- Certificate of no marriage (in some countries)
- Get I-134 affidavit of support from U.S. petitioner (with tax documents of U.S. petitioner)
- Learn about the U.S. state they will live in with the U.S. petitioner
- Learn about the U.S. petitioner's financial situation, living conditions, previous marriages, and criminal past (if any)

Step 2. References:

"I-129F, Petition for Alien Fiancé(e)." USCIS, 5 May 2018, https://www.uscis.gov/i-129f

"National Visa Center." U.S. Department of State - Bureau of Consular Affairs, 9 May 2018, https://travel.state.gov/content/travel/en/us-visas/immigrate/national-visa-center.html

"NVC Contact Information." U.S. Department of State - Bureau of Consular Affairs, 9 May 2018, https://travel.state.gov/content/travel/en/us-visas/immigrate/national-visa-center/nvc-contact-information.html

"Form I-129F Instructions." USCIS, 5 May 2018, https://www.uscis.gov/sites/default/files/files/form/i-129finstr.pdf

"Form I-797: Types and Functions." USCIS, 5 May 2018, https://www.uscis.gov/i-797-info

"Case Status Online." USCIS, 5 May 2018, https://egov.uscis.gov/casestatus/landing.do

Step 3. Embassy Prep

Step 3.0 - Embassy Preparation

At this point, the U.S. petitioner has called the National Visa Center to the get the case number or the National Visa Center has sent a letter to the U.S. petitioner with the case number. The National Visa Center sent the approved package to the U.S. embassy nearest to the foreign fiancé(e).

Once the U.S. embassy gets the approved I-129F package, they are supposed to mail the foreign fiancé(e) a list of what they need, where to go for medical, and what to do next. Sometimes (for whatever reason) this does not get to the foreign fiancé(e) or it takes a long time to get to them. But for most of what needs to be done, there is no need to wait. The foreign fiancé(e) can start now with this checklist:

Embassy Prep Checklist (part 1)

Embassy Preparation Checklist	
Tasks/Documents	
Open Communication With fiancé(e). Make sure you and your fiancé(e) have a legit relationship. You should know each other's personal history and talk openly and honestly about what happened with past marriages and criminal history. The consular officer may ask about these things in the interview.	
A copy of Nonimmigrant visa electronic confirmation page (DS-160). Complete the DS-160 and print the DS-160 Confirmation Page that contains the barcode information to bring to your interview. This is needed to get into the U.S. embassy. https://ceac.state.gov/genniv/	
Medical Results from Medical Examination. All K-1 and K-2 visa applicants must complete a medical examination at the U.S. immigration approved physician or facility. Medical results will be given to the U.S. embassy directly or delivered by the foreign fiancé(e) during the interview (see Step 4 for more details).	
Passport. The foreign fiancé(e) must have a passport that is valid for at least 6 months at the time of the interview.	
A certified copy of Birth Certificate. Obtain a certified original copy (not an extract) of the birth certificate from the local registrar and/or country where the foreign fiancé(e) was born (get at least 3 - 4 originals because they will be needed again especially for kids going to USA).	
A certified copy of police certificate/clearance. The foreign fiancé(e) should get a police certificate from the local government. This may have different names. For example, this is called a National Bureau of Investigation (NBI) clearance in the Philippines.	

Figure, Step 3 Checklist (part1). Communicating with your fiancé is important for embassy preparation. It is important not only to review the checklist together you should also discuss the direction of your relationship, financial issues, and your past. A real relationship is a requirement of the K-1 interview. If you communicate often, there will be little issues with proving your relationship is real.

Embassy Prep Checklist (part 2)

A copy of Other Country Police Certificates. Applicant aged 16 years and older must also present police certificates from other countries where they have lived for six (6) months or more after reaching the age of 16. Foreign police certificates should be obtained in any maiden names, aliases or nicknames used while in the country in question, including different spellings you have used of those names.	
Copies of Court and Prison Records. Applicants who had been arrested, charged or convicted of a crime must present copies or transcripts of court or prison records relating to the crime or offense.	
Certified copies of Military or Police Service Records. Applicants who served in the military or police should present certified copies of their military or police service records.	
Evidence of a Genuine Engagement. A foreign fiancé(e) must be prepared to prove to the consular officer that they have a genuine relationship with the petitioner. Samples could include: screenshot of chat messages, chat logs, photographs, letters, emails, phone records, bank records and remittance records as evidence supporting the relationship and an updated letter of intent to marry.	
Proof of Meeting. Evidence of meeting in person could include pictures together, ticket and/or receipts with names, dates, locations.	

Figure, Step 3 Checklist (part 2).

During the embassy preparation, the foreign fiancé will need to go to local government agencies to gather police records and military records (if they have ever serviced in the military. Some of the proof of meeting should already be available if the U.S. petitioner saved any of the previous evidence that was given the USICS.

Embassy Prep Checklist (part 3)

Letters of Intent to Marry. Create evidence of intention to marry within 90 days of arrival in the USA signed by the U.S. petitioner and foreign fiancé(e).	
A certified copy of Proof of Termination of a Prior Marriage. If applicable, official documents (divorce decree, annulment decree or death certificate, etc.) that prove all prior marriages contracted by the foreign fiancé(e) and the petitioner have been legally terminated prior to the I-129F.	
*NOT IN ALL COUNTRIES - **Certified copy of Certificate of No Marriage Record (CENOMAR).** The U.S. embassy will let the foreign fiancé(e) know if they need this. **This is not applicable in most countries.** (Philippines) If the foreign fiancé(e) has never been married, a CENOMAR (singleness) issued by the National Statistics Office (NSO) and printed on NSO security paper must be submitted. NSO contact number:02-737-1111 **http://census.gov.ph/**	
Evidence of Support. The U.S. petitioner must be able to demonstrate that they make enough income to support the foreign fiancé(e) so they do not become a public charge or be a burden on the U.S. taxpayers for financial support. A completed I-134 Affidavit of Support with an original signature will be useful to the consular officer to evaluate your petitioner's ability to be financially responsible for you. The foreign fiancé(e) should submit their petitioner's most recent U.S. Federal Income Tax Return (Form 1040) and wage statements (Form W-2). Employment letters stating the salaries and bank statements may be included to substantiate the I-134. More information on the I-134: **http://www.uscis.gov/i-134**. See poverty guideline for income. http://aspe.hhs.gov	

Figure, Step 3 Checklist (part 3).

The foreign fiancé will need signed letters of intent to marry from both themselves and the U.S. petitioner. They will also need to gather copies of divorce decrees, annulments, or death certificates (if there were previous marriages from either them or the U.S. petitioner).

Embassy Prep Checklist (part 4)

Evidence of Ongoing Support. Receipts of the U.S. petitioner sending financial support to the foreign fiancé(e).	
4 pcs visa photos. Prepare (4) visa photos. (2) may be taken during the U.S. embassy interview, and another (2) for the medical report. Photos should be 2 by 2 inches (roughly 50 mm square passport style photos) with white background and the head centered in the frame.	
DHS documents (if applicable). If the foreign fiancé(e) has applied for any benefit such as change of status, adjustment of status, or asylum, before United States Citizenship and Immigration Services (USCIS), or have been the subject of any enforcement proceedings, such as deportation or removal proceedings by ICE Immigration and Customs Enforcement, bring all your documents pertaining to such matters with you to the interview.	
Visa Application Fee & Schedule Visa Interview. The U.S. embassy will send instruction on how the fiancé can pay for and schedule the visa interview. They can also get information here: www.ustraveldocs.com/	

Figure, Step 3 Checklist (part 4). Some embassies ask for evidence of ongoing support. This is different from "evidence of support". Evidence of ONGOING support includes things like copies of MoneyGram or Western Union receipts to show that the U.S. petitioner has sent financial support to their foreign fiancé. Evidence of Support is different because it uses Form I-134, affidavit of support, U.S. tax forms and financial statements to prove that the U.S. petitioner makes enough income to care for the foreign fiancé once they get to the USA.

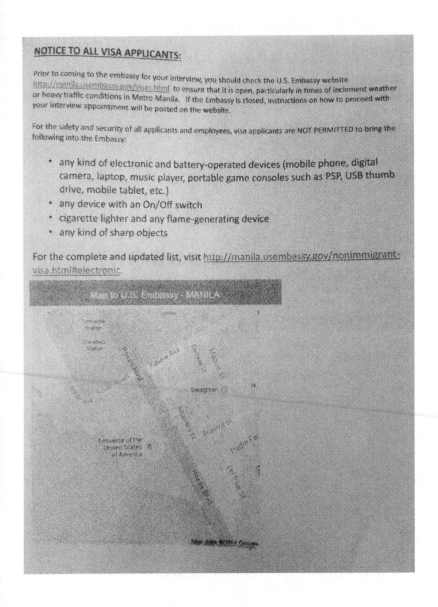

NOTICE TO ALL VISA APPLICANTS:

Prior to coming to the embassy for your interview, you should check the U.S. Embassy website http://manila.usembassy.gov/visas.html to ensure that it is open, particularly in times of inclement weather or heavy traffic conditions in Metro Manila. If the Embassy is closed, instructions on how to proceed with your interview appointment will be posted on the website.

For the safety and security of all applicants and employees, visa applicants are NOT PERMITTED to bring the following into the Embassy:

* any kind of electronic and battery-operated devices (mobile phone, digital camera, laptop, music player, portable game consoles such as PSP, USB thumb drive, mobile tablet, etc.)
* any device with an On/Off switch
* cigarette lighter and any flame-generating device
* any kind of sharp objects

For the complete and updated list, visit http://manila.usembassy.gov/nonimmigrant-visa.html#electronic.

Map to U.S. Embassy - MANILA

Figure, a sample page of instructions from an embassy

Once the I-129F package is approved and sent from NVC to the embassy, the U.S. embassy will send mail to the foreign fiancé(e) with detailed instructions on what is needed, what to do, and where to go.

Step 3.1 - Embassy Preparation DS-160

The foreign fiancé(e) will need to fill out the online form called the DS-160. The DS-160, Online Nonimmigrant Visa Application form is for temporary travel to the United States, and for "K" fiancé(e) visas. The foreign fiancé(e) will need to upload a copy of their passport style photo in the DS-160 when asked to do so.

Form DS-160 is submitted electronically to the Department of State and accessed directly from the Internet. Consular officers use the information entered on the DS-160 to process the visa application and, combined with a personal interview, determine an applicant's eligibility for a nonimmigrant visa. The U.S. petitioner can help with this form, but the foreign fiancé(e) must digitally sign it and print it out. The DS-160 Online Nonimmigrant Visa Application is located at:

- https://ceac.state.gov/genniv/

The DS-160 asks the foreign fiancé(e) biographical information, work history, residential questions, questions about family, and questions that assist with a security background check. Sections of the DS-160 include, but are not limited to:

- Personal Information
- Address and Phone Information
- Travel Information
- U.S. Point of Contact Information
- Family Information
- Previous Work/Education/Training Information
- Security and Background
- Upload Photo
- Preparer of Application
- Signature
- Confirmation Page

#YuriBruce: Visa Approved series

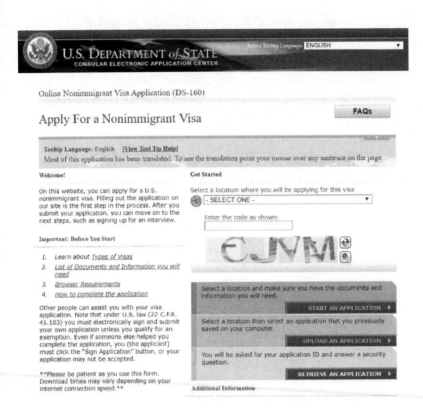

Figure, DS-160 Online Nonimmigrant Visa Application

https://ceac.state.gov/genniv/

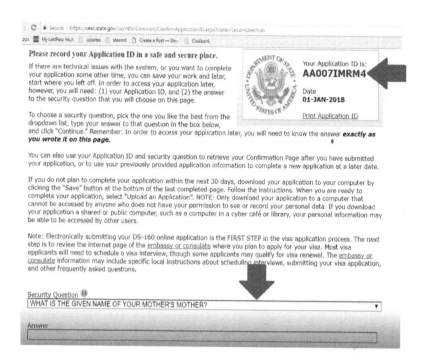

Figure, DS-160 Application ID

The DS-160 application ID allows the applicant to save their work and start where they left off if there is a technical issue. The applicant has to have the application ID and answer the security questions.

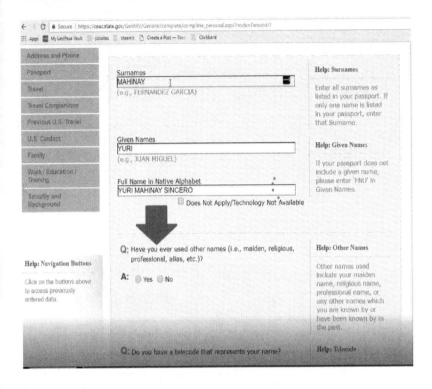

Figure, Set up DS-160
DS-160 requires the foreign fiancé(e)'s name and other names used (such as maiden names from previous marriages).

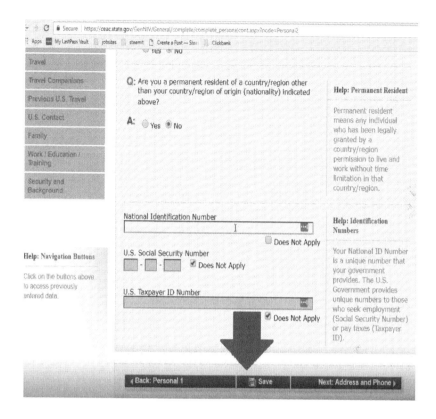

Figure, Set-up and Save the DS-160

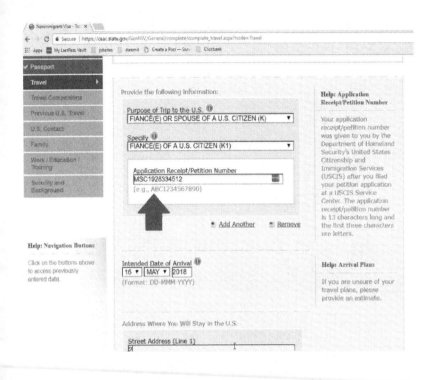

Figure, Add the application receipt/Petition Number to DS-160

The application receipt/Petition number is given to the petitioner by the USCIS on the Notice of Action approval (NOA2) and Notice of Action Receipt (NOA1). It is 13 characters long and starts with three letters.

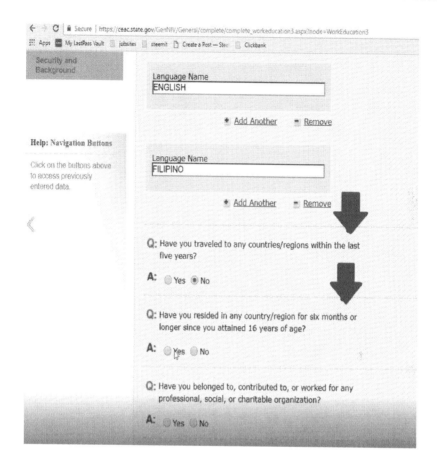

Figure, DS-160 Asks About Travel

#YuriBruce: Visa Approved series

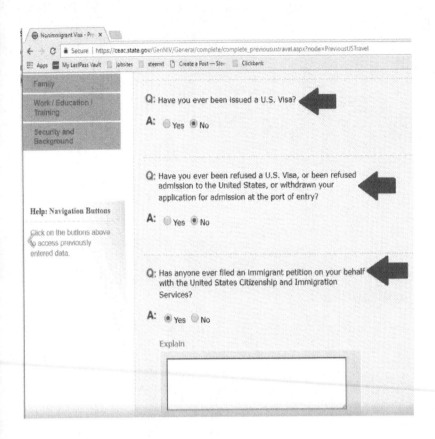

Figure, DS-160 question about past U.S. visas

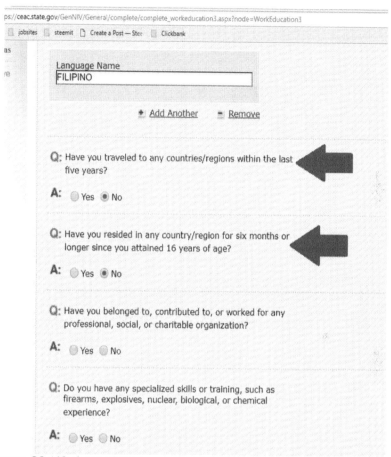

Language Name
FILIPINO

✚ Add Another   ▬ Remove

Q: Have you traveled to any countries/regions within the last five years?

A: ○ Yes ⦿ No

Q: Have you resided in any country/region for six months or longer since you attained 16 years of age?

A: ○ Yes ⦿ No

Q: Have you belonged to, contributed to, or worked for any professional, social, or charitable organization?

A: ○ Yes ○ No

Q: Do you have any specialized skills or training, such as firearms, explosives, nuclear, biological, or chemical experience?

A: ○ Yes ○ No

Figure, DS-160 about travel to any countries/regions

#YuriBruce: Visa Approved series

Figure, Security and Background

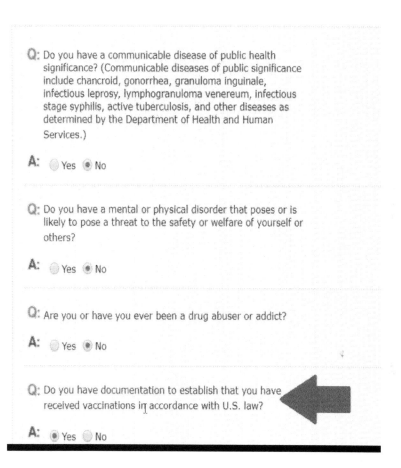

Q: Do you have a communicable disease of public health significance? (Communicable diseases of public significance include chancroid, gonorrhea, granuloma inguinale, infectious leprosy, lymphogranuloma venereum, infectious stage syphilis, active tuberculosis, and other diseases as determined by the Department of Health and Human Services.)

A: ○ Yes ● No

Q: Do you have a mental or physical disorder that poses or is likely to pose a threat to the safety or welfare of yourself or others?

A: ○ Yes ● No

Q: Are you or have you ever been a drug abuser or addict?

A: ○ Yes ● No

Q: Do you have documentation to establish that you have received vaccinations in accordance with U.S. law?

A: ● Yes ○ No

Figure, DS-160 questions about drugs and vaccinations

#YuriBruce: Visa Approved series

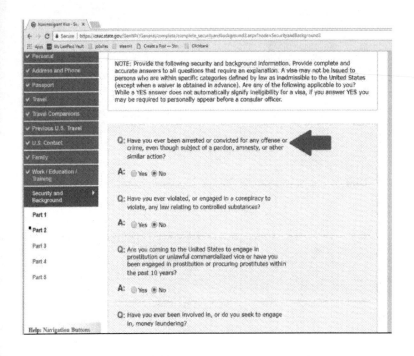

Figure, DS-160 Crimes and Conviction

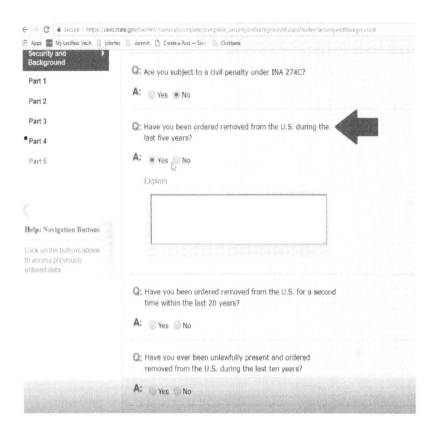

Figure, DS-160 More Questions on Security and Background

After Completing the DS-160

After you have completed the DS-160, you must take the following steps:

- **Print and Keep the DS-160 Confirmation Page.** The foreign fiancé(e) will need to print the confirmation page and keep it to enter the U.S. embassy.
- **Schedule the Embassy Interview.** Petitioner and/or foreign fiancé(e) must schedule a visa interview appointment for the foreign fiancé(e). Unless otherwise directed, the U.S. embassy or Consulate does not schedule an appointment for you. Visit the U.S. Embassy or Consulate website where you will be interviewed for country-specific instructions (see Step 3.8).
- **Pay the Visa Application Processing Fee**. Review country-specific instructions on the U.S. Embassy or Consulate website.

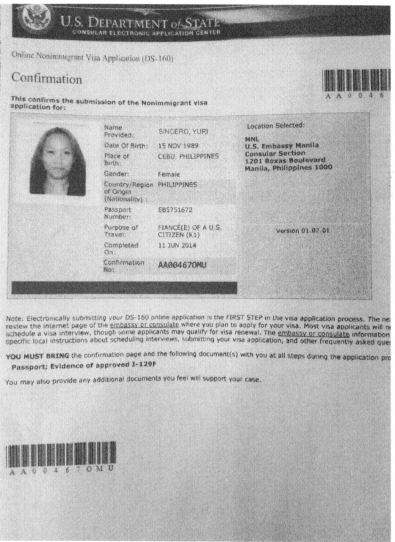

Figure, Actual Sample DS-160 Confirmation Page

The foreign fiancé(e) must print out the DS-160 confirmation page. This is necessary to enter the embassy.

Step 3.2 - Embassy Preparation - Important Papers

The foreign fiancé(e) needs to start preparing what will be needed for the embassy interview. This step will focus on the following things the foreign fiancé(e) will need:

- DS-160 Confirmation Page
- PASSPORT
- (3 - 4) Birth Certificates (original)
- (4) Visa/passport style photo
- Certificate of No Marriage (if applicable)
- End of previous marriage (if applicable)
- Department of Homeland Security (DHS) Documents (if applicable)

DS-160 Confirmation Page

Once the foreign fiancé(e) has completed the DS-160 online application, there will be a confirmation page at the very end. It will have a barcode and a picture of the foreign fiancé(e). Print that page out. It is used as a ticket to enter the U.S. Embassy.

Figure, DS-160 Print Confirmation page

Passport

The foreign fiancé(e) must have a passport from their home country that is valid for at least 6 months at the time of K-1 visa approval. For those who have never left their home country and are not sure how international travel works, you need a passport which is an international ID attached to a booklet. Once the foreign fiancé(e) is approved, the U.S. State Department will give them a sort of sticker ID placed inside the passport booklet that allows entry into the USA. This is called a visa. A visa is needed for citizens of some countries to enter certain countries based on international agreements. For example, citizens from the Philippines need a visa to enter the USA, but citizens of the UK need to go through the Electronic System for Travel Authorization (ESTA) application to enter the USA (72 hours before departure as of 2018).

(4) Visa/Passport Style Photo

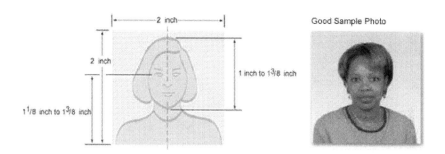

Figure, Visa Style Photo

A visa style photo is the same as a passport style photo. The foreign fiancé(e) should get 4 visa/passport style photos. Some may be needed at the medical exam and at the embassy interview. The visa style photo must be:

- In Color
- Sized such that the head is between 1 inch and 1 3/8 inches (22 mm and 35 mm) or 50% and 69% of the image's total height from the bottom of the chin to the top of the head.
- Taken within the last 6 months to reflect your current appearance
- Taken in front of a plain white or off-white background
- Just like the Passport style photo

(3-4) Original Copy of Birth Certificate

We recommend the foreign fiancé(e) get 3 -4 original copies of their birth certificate. The U.S. embassy may take one during the interview. You should have a few spares just in case they don't give the birth certificate back. The foreign fiancé(e) will need more when they move to the United States so it is better to have more than needed than less. If the foreign fiancé has children, bring multiple originals for them as well because original birth certificates may be hard to get once they are living in the U.S.

Provide Evidence that Previous Marriages Have Ended (if applicable)

If the foreign fiancé(e) or petitioner have ever been married before, they have to provide documents that show that all previous marriages have ended. Evidence that the old relationships ended include official copies of divorce decrees, annulments, or death certificates.

CENOMAR (Certificate of No Marriage) (only if asked)

Most countries do not have this. But for those that do, the U.S. embassy will ask for a certificate of NO Marriage (also known as a certificate of singleness). For example, the Embassy in Manila does ask for this, but the one in the Dominican Republic does not.

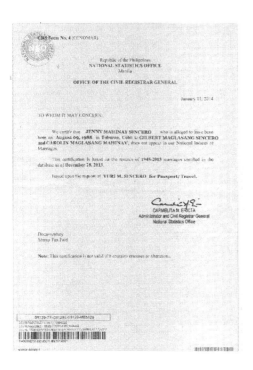

Figure, Certificate of No Marriage

Department of Homeland Security Documents (if applicable)

This is not applicable to most foreign fiancé(e)s. If the foreign fiancé(e) has applied for any benefit such as U.S. immigrant change of status, adjustment of status (U.S. immigrant), or asylum in the U.S., or has been the subject of any enforcement proceedings, such as deportation or removal proceedings by U.S. Immigration and Customs Enforcement, please bring all documents pertaining to such matters to the interview.

Step 3.3 - Embassy Preparation - Evidence of Engagement

When the foreign fiancé(e) goes to the U.S. embassy for the interview, the consular officer may ask about how they got engaged. They may ask about the proposal, when the wedding will be held, where it will be, and who is invited.

The couple does not need exact dates, times, and locations of their wedding, but they should have a plan on how and when they will get married. For example, if they have discussed just going to the courthouse and getting a marriage license rather than a marriage, then the foreign fiancé(e) can just explain that. If the couple has wedding invitations, they can bring them.

If the petitioner and foreign fiancé(e) don't have any idea when it will be but know for sure it will be within 90 days of the fiancé(e)'s entry into the USA, they can do a "letter of intent to marry". In the letter of intent (from the U.S. petitioner and foreign fiancé(e)) explain that you will get married to each other within 90 days of arriving in the USA, sign the document, and bring it to the U.S. embassy interview. You can also use the letters of intent you provided in the I-129F.

Aside from the wedding invitations, and the letter of intent to marry within 90 days, we have heard of fiancé(e)s showing their ring or the receipt for the engagement ring, but we used the letter of intent.

Figure, Letter of Intent from Beneficiary

Yuri Sincero
#18 Manga St Opra Blvd
Cebu City, Philippines 6000
pinalove24@gmail.com

United States Department of Homeland Security
U.S. Citizenship and Immigration Services
Attn: I-129F
2501 South State Highway 121 Business
Suite 400
Lewisville, TX 75067

25 April 2014

Dear Sir or Madam:

I, Yuri M. Sincero, do hereby state that I am legally able and willing to marry Bruce Brown. I intend to do so within 90 days of my arrival to the US using the K-1 visa.

Being away from the man that I really love has been very hard and lonely. I have been ready to start a joyous home with him. His love has given me contentment and satisfaction in life beyond material things. I am very thankful that I found my match. I am very proud of having a great man and I am so honored that he would have me as his wife.

Yours truly,
yuriS
Yuri Sincero

Dear Sir or Madam:

I, Bruce Brown, do hereby state that I am legally able and willing to marry Yuri Sincero. I intend to do so within 90 days of her arrival to the US using the K-1 visa.

Being away from her has caused me great heartache. I am ready to start a new life with her. She makes me very happy. I am very blessed to have found such an amazing match. I am honored that she would have me as her husband.

Yours truly,

Bruce Brown
Bruce Brown

Figure, Letter of Intent from U.S. Petition

Step 3.4 - Embassy Preparation - Important Records

There are some records that the foreign fiancé(e) will need to gather before the U.S. embassy interview. These records will require some running around from place to place and research from the foreign fiancé(e) because these records are in their country. These records include:

- Police Certificate
- Other Country Police Certificates
- Court and Prison Records
- Military or Police Service Records

Police Certificate

The foreign fiancé(e) must get this document from their home country. It is sometimes called police clearance or police verification. It is an official document issued as a result of a background check by the local police or government agency of a country. This would include a criminal record if there is one.

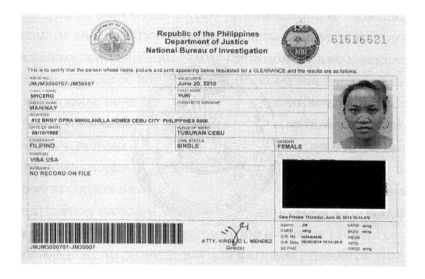

Figure, Police Clearance

A Copy of Other Country Police Certificates (if applicable)

Foreign fiancé(e)s must also present police certificates from other countries where they have lived for six (6) months or more. Foreign police certificates should be obtained in any maiden names, aliases, or nicknames used while in the country in question, including different spellings the foreign fiancé(e)s have used of those names.

An example of who this would apply to would be an Indian national working in Qatar who is going through the K-1 fiancé(e) visa process. They would need to get a police clearance from Qatar if they had worked there for (6) months or more. Depending on the country, the process of getting the clearance can take days, weeks, or months which can affect the K-1 process.

This is for beneficiaries aged 16 years and older who have lived abroad.

Figure, Police Clearance from Another County

Copies of Court and Prison Records

If the foreign fiancé(e) has been arrested, charged, or convicted of a crime they must present copies or transcripts of court or prison records relating to the crime or offense. It is better to be truthful with this because the U.S. embassy can easily find out if the foreign fiancé(e) has been arrested or been in jail. Being arrested or serving time in jail does not mean the foreign fiancé(e) will be automatically denied. The consular officer must make a determination based on the data presented.

Record: 1 of 2   Forward 1 record   Last record

RefNo	Title	Date
JC8	High Court Minute Books - Series E 1799-1899	

CountryCode	GB
RepCode	234
RefNo	JC8:20
Repository	National Archives of Scotland
Title	Minute Book
Date	6 Mar 1826-27 Nov 1826
Accused	Peter Moffat, junior, weaver, Address: Kilsyth, Stirlingshire. Entry relating to the crime of murder. Tried at High Court, Edinburgh. Date of trial: 26 Jun 1826, Verdict: Guilty, Sentence: Death - hanging by public executioner, Note: Executed at Stirling, 28 July 1826
Accused	James McIntosh, clerk, Stirling Post Office. Entry relating to the crime of theft at Stirling. Date of trial: 17 Jul 1826, Verdict: Guilty, Verdict Comments: Guilty in terms of own confession, Sentence: Transportation - 7 years
Accused	William Mason, nailer. Entry relating to the crime of illegal killing of game at Duddingston woods, Abercorn, Linlithgow. Date of trial: 20 Mar 1826, Verdict: Guilty, Verdict Comments: Guilty in terms of own confession, Sentence: Imprisonment - 3 months

Figure, Court Record Copy

Certified Copies of Military or Police Service Records

Foreign fiancé(e)s who served in the military or as police officers need to present certified copies of their military or police service records. This documentation is usually provided by the military or police department once service is complete. This can be a photocopy unless the U.S. embassy asks for an original.

Step 3.5 - Embassy Preparation Evidence of Ongoing Relationship

In the U.S. embassy interview, one of the biggest things they focus on is your relationship. We know that they need evidence that you are engaged and you prove that with an "intent to marry" document. But they also want to know if you have a real ongoing relationship. You will need to provide:

- Evidence of Ongoing Relationship
- Evidence of Support

Evidence of Ongoing Relationship

For evidence of an ongoing relationship, you should have at least three pictures together, and copies of your chat logs or phone logs. Phone logs can be a list of phone calls between the U.S. petitioner and the foreign fiancé(e).
If the petitioner and foreign fiancé(e) chat online using Facebook messenger, get screenshots of the chat session. Give them chat logs of whatever software you used. If e-mail was used, provide copies of your e-mail messages that establish there was a relationship.

The foreign fiancé(e) should bring 5 - 10 pages of recent and old chats. Here is an example of chat logs in "Figure, Chat logs from Hangouts 1" which is a copy of chats from Google Hangouts and Gmail, but you must provide screenshots and/or logs from whatever you and your fiancé(e) used to communicate.

Figure, Chat logs From Hangouts

#YuriBruce: Visa Approved series

Figure, Chat logs From Hangouts 2

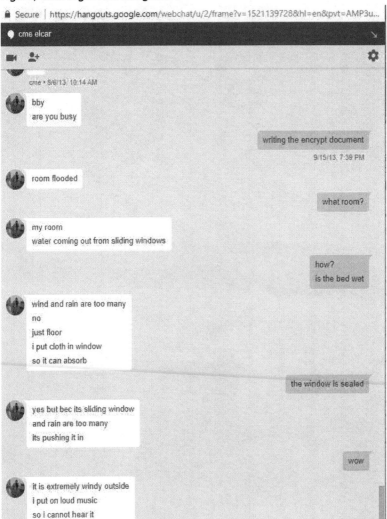

Evidence of Ongoing Support

The U.S. embassy may ask for evidence of ongoing support. Examples of evidence of support could be receipts from Western Union, Xoom, PayPal, MoneyGram or other money sending services.

If the U.S. petitioner has ever sent money to the foreign fiancé(e), you want to provide proof with receipts.

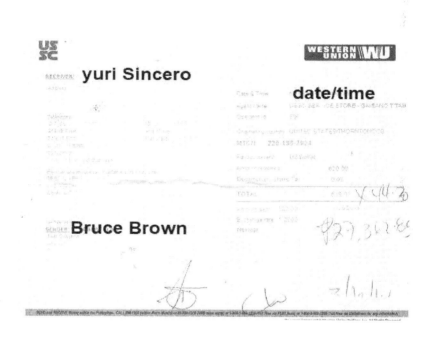

Figure, Evidence of Ongoing Support

In addition to evidence of ongoing support, the couple will need to provide evidence of support for the foreign fiancé(e) once they are in the USA. This is done with a Form I-134, Affidavit of Support discussed later.

Pictures, Pictures, Pictures

In Step 1, Petition Package, the U.S. petitioner should have already established the dates that they met the foreign fiancé(e) along with evidence and pictures. The foreign fiancé(e) should match the same time frame and provide supporting pictures of them together. We recommend at least three pictures. They can be the same ones submitted with the I-129F or different pictures.

Figure, Picture in Thailand

Figure, Picture in Hong Kong

Figure, Picture in Cebu Philippines

Figure, Picture together with Thailand in the background

Step 3.6 – Embassy Preparation – Evidence of Support

Evidence of support means that the U.S. petitioner must be able to demonstrate that the foreign fiancé(e) will not become a public charge or be a burden on the U.S. taxpayers for financial support. A public charge means welfare.

I-134, Affidavit of Support (from U.S. Petitioner)

The U.S. petitioner must provide the foreign fiancé(e) with a form I-134, Affidavit of Support. On this form, the petitioner is called the "sponsor" of the foreign fiancé(e) (also known as a beneficiary on the I-134). This form can also be done by a co-sponsor if the petitioner does not make equal to or greater than the U.S. poverty.

This document must have the signature of the U.S. petitioner or co-sponsor. This form is used by the consular officer to evaluate the petitioner's ability to be financially responsible for the foreign fiancé(e) /beneficiary.

Affidavit of Support	USCIS
Department of Homeland Security U.S. Citizenship and Immigration Services	Form I-134 OMB No. 1615-0014 Expires 11/30/2018

► **START HERE** - Type or print in black ink.

Part 1. Information About You (the Sponsor)

Your Full Name

1.a. Family Name (Last Name)

1.b. Given Name (First Name)

1.c. Middle Name

Other Names Used

List all other names you have ever used, including aliases, maiden name, and nicknames. If you need extra space to complete this section, use the space provided in **Part 7. Additional Information.**

2.a. Family Name (Last Name)

2.b. Given Name (First Name)

2.c. Middle Name

Sponsor's Mailing Address

3.a. In Care Of Name

3.b. Street Number and Name

3.c. ☐ Apt. ☐ Ste. ☐ Flr.

3.d. City or Town

3.e. State ☐ 3.f. ZIP Code

3.g. Province

3.h. Postal Code

3.i. Country

4. Are your mailing address and physical address the same? ☐ Yes ☐ No

Sponsor's Physical Address

5.a. Street Number and Name

5.b. ☐ Apt. ☐ Ste. ☐ Flr.

5.c. City or Town

5.d. State 5.e. ZIP Code

5.f. Province

5.g. Postal Code

5.h. Country

Other Information

6. Date of Birth (mm/dd/yyyy)

7.a. Town or City of Birth

7.b. Country of Birth

8. Alien Registration Number (A-Number) (if any) ► A-

9. U.S. Social Security Number (if any) ►

10. USCIS Online Account Number (if any) ►

Citizenship or Residency or Status

If you are not a U.S. citizen based on your birth in the United States, or a non-citizen U.S. national based on your birth in American Samoa (including Swains Island), answer the following as appropriate:

11.a. ☐ I am a U.S. citizen through naturalization. My Certificate of Naturalization number is

Figure, I-134 Affidavit of Support

http://www.uscis.gov/i-134

"Section 212(a)(4) of the Immigration and Nationality Act **(INA) bars the admission into the United States of any foreign national** who, in the opinion of the U.S. Department of State officer adjudicating a visa application, ... **is likely at any time to become a public charge.**"

General Information About Filling Out the I-134

Make sure the U.S. petitioner signs the Form I-134. They can submit a photocopy if it is legible. **In some cases, the U.S. embassy will ask for the original document that the U.S. petitioner signed (wet ink).** If the foreign fiancé(e) has children, they will need to be listed on the I-134 to get a K-2 visa.

There is no fee for filing the I-134. The form must be in English (or translated to English if originally done in another language). The form is filled out, signed by the U.S. petitioner, and sent to the foreign fiancé(e) along with supporting documents.

Supporting documents will be evidence that the U.S. petitioner makes at or above the poverty line of the USA (according to the state and household size):

- Petitioner's most recent U.S. Federal Income Tax Return (Form 1040 or 1099)
- Wage statements (form W-2)
- Employment letters stating the salaries
- Bank statements may be included to substantiate the I-134
- Must make 100% of the U.S. poverty line for their household size and state
- If there is another source of income, provide documentation as proof

100% of the Poverty Guideline Explained

The consular officer will compare the U.S. petitioner's income with the poverty guideline (*https://aspe.hhs.gov/poverty-guidelines*). They use this to determine if the U.S. petitioner will be financially capable of taking care of the foreign fiancé(e) when they arrive to the United States.

    The U.S. petitioner must have enough income and assets to equal at least 100% of the poverty line for their household size. For example, if their household size is three people (U.S. petitioner, foreign fiancé(e), +1 child) and they will live in Arkansas, they must make $20,780 USD per year (as of 2018 – see *https://aspe.hhs.gov/poverty-guidelines*). For another example, if the U.S. petitioner makes $17,000 per year and there will be four people in the household once the foreign fiancé(e) arrives in the state of Texas, then the U.S. petitioner does not make enough.

HHS POVERTY GUIDELINES FOR 2018

The 2018 poverty guidelines are in effect as of January 13, 2018.
See also the Federal Register notice of the 2018 poverty guidelines, published January 18, 2018

2018 POVERTY GUIDELINES FOR THE 48 CONTIGUOUS STATES AND THE DISTRICT OF COLUMBIA	
PERSONS IN FAMILY/HOUSEHOLD	POVERTY GUIDELINE
For families/households with more than 8 persons, add $4,320 for each additional person.	
1	$12,140
2	$16,460
3	$20,780
4	$25,100
5	$29,420
6	$33,740
7	$38,060
8	$42,380

2018 POVERTY GUIDELINES FOR ALASKA	*Note: AK & HI different*
PERSONS IN FAMILY/HOUSEHOLD	POVERTY GUIDELINE

Figure, U.S. Department of Health & Human Services Poverty Guidelines
https://aspe.hhs.gov/poverty-guidelines (changes annually)

What if the U.S. Petitioner Does NOT Make Enough?

If the U.S. petitioner does not make enough income, they may want to consider a few options:

- **Use a co-sponsor – friend, relative or associate of the U.S. petitioner willing to help financially**
  o Have another U.S. citizen fill out and sign an additional I-134
  o Provide co-sponsor's income verification evidence (W2, 1099), 1040, or individual tax return transcript (ITR)
  o BOTH U.S. petitioner AND co-sponsor must fill out the I-134 as a sponsor
  o This option is at the discretion of the consular officer and there is no guarantee it will be accepted
- **Get another job or source of income to make enough**
  o With supporting evidence of income (income verification: earning statement or W2)
- **Do not start the process until the U.S. citizen makes enough or has enough assets that meet or exceed the poverty guideline**

How to Fill Out Form I-134, Affidavit of Support

There are few things to remember while filling out the form:

- Use black ink, print or type legibly
- For no answer – Type or print "N/A" – If the information is Not Applicable
- If the numerical response is zero, put "0" or print or type "None"
- Use "Additional Information" or extra pages if you need more space
- Don't forget the signature of the petitioner

Part 1. Information About the Petitioner (I-134)

Part 1 asks basic information about the U.S. petitioner. The full name, address (physical and mailing), date of birth, Alien Registration number (if applicable), U.S. Social Security Number (if any), USCIS Online Account Number (if any). Part 1 also asks about the U.S. petitioner's citizenship status.

Part 2. Information About the Beneficiary (I-134)

Part 2 focuses on basic information about the beneficiary. The form calls for the full name, date of birth, gender, Alien registration number (if any), country of citizenship/nationality, marital status, and relationship to the sponsor (U.S. petitioner or co-sponsor).

Beneficiary's Physical Address. Provide the street number and name of the beneficiary's physical address. In some cases, the address is so long that the sponsor may need to print the document and write the address in with a pen (using black ink) or provide the full address on an additional page. The address should be written in English.

Beneficiary's Spouse (not for K-1 visas). This is not for K-1 fiancé(e)ss as they should not be married. K-1 applicants can put "N/A" or leave it blank. Form I-134, Affidavit of Support is also used for family visas. In these cases, the beneficiary may have an accompanying spouse.

Beneficiary's Children. Provide the full name, birthday, and gender of all the beneficiary's children. Form I-134 has two entries for children (Child 1 and Child 2); however, you can add more children on the part of the I-134 labeled "Additional Information" or on a blank page. If there are no children, print or type N/A or leave it blank.

Part 3. Other Information About the Sponsor (Employment & Assets) (I-134)

Employment Information

Indicate if the petitioner is employed or self-employed, and type or print the petitioner's profession, employer, and/or business. Provide additional positions and/or businesses on the "Additional Information" section or on additional sheets of paper.

Part 3. Other Information About the Sponsor
Employment Information

I am currently:

1.a. ☐ Employed as a/an [_____]

1.a.1. Name of Employer (if applicable)
[_____]

1.b. ☐ Self employed as a/an
[_____]

Figure, Employment Information

Employed

If the U.S. petitioner is employed, provide the street name and number of the employer in "Current Employer Address". The U.S. petitioner will also need to provide a statement from their employer that has the following information:

- Date and nature of employment
- Salary paid
- Whether the position is temporary or permanent
- *the U.S. embassy sometimes asks for more

Self-Employed

If the petitioner is self-employed, they will need to provide the following:

- Copy of last income tax return filed
- Report of commercial rating concern
- *the U.S. embassy sometimes asks for more

Income Verification with Tax

The U.S. embassy will ask for income tax documents. Provide the most recent tax documentation. The U.S. petitioner can

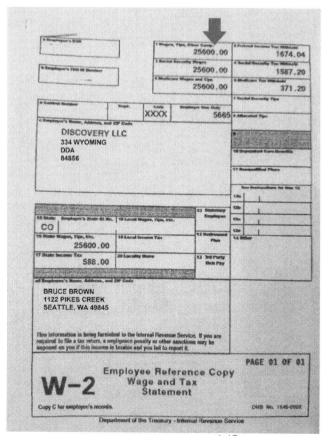

143

get Individual Tax Return Transcripts directly from the IRS if needed.

- Applicable tax documents (W2, 1040, 1099)

Figure, W-2

Tax documentation will be needed as evidence that the U.S. petitioner makes enough income to support the foreign national that they will sponsor. Examples of tax documents include: W-2, 1040, and/or 1099

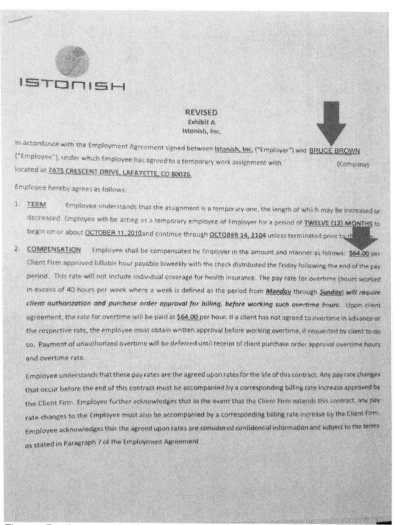

Figure, Employment Verification

Employment verification may be a contract or a simple letter with the company letterhead, date of employment, and the amount that the U.S. petitioner makes.

Income and Asset Information

The key to the income and asset information section is to provide evidence that the U.S. petitioner has at least 100% of the U.S. poverty level in the U.S. That means the petitioner must make equal to or greater than the U.S. poverty line in their state according to the number of people in their household who are in their financial care *(see the current U.S. poverty line: https://aspe.hhs.gov/poverty-guidelines).* In some cases, the petitioner's income is short but their assets (homes, securities, investments, savings, personal property etc.) are enough to supplement their annual income. This determination is in the hands of the U.S. consular officer. So, the best thing the petitioner can do is to provide as much evidence as possible that they have enough income and assets to care for their household (including the foreign fiancé(e)).

Income and Asset Information

3. My annual income is $ [   ]

(If self-employed, I have attached a copy of my last income tax return or report of commercial rating concern which I certify to be true and correct to the best of my knowledge and belief. See Instructions for nature of evidence of net worth to be submitted.)

4. Balance of all my savings and checking accounts in United States-based financial institutions
                                      $ [   ]

5. Value of my other personal property
                                      $ [   ]

6. Market value of my stocks and bonds
                                      $ [   ]

I have listed my stocks and bonds in **Part 7. Additional Information** (or attached a list of them), which I certify to be true and correct to the best of my knowledge and belief.

Figure, Income and Asset Information

NOTE: The petitioner cannot include income from welfare and food stamps.

Annual Income

Add the annual income of the U.S. petitioner in the "Income and Asset Information" section. The U.S. petitioner will need to attach their most recent income tax returns, W2, a statement from their employer on business stationery showing income and position (for employed petitioners). Form I-134 instructions mention providing a report of commercial rating or tax documents for the self-employed.

Bank Statement, Financial Institutions, and Evidence (if applicable)

Add current balance of the petitioner's saving and checking accounts in U.S. financial institutions. Evidence of the balance will be a statement from the financial institutions. This could be a print out of bank deposits that shows when the account was open, total amount deposited in the last year, and present balance.

Value of Petitioner's Personal Property (if applicable)

Add the value of the petitioner's personal property. No evidence is required for the personal property. Personal property does not refer to real estate. Personal property includes but is not limited to: Electronics, jewelry, furniture, vehicles, merchandise such as clothes, dishes, toys, animals. Estimate the value of all these items and add the amount to Form I-134 under "personal property".

Market Value of Petitioner's Stocks, Bonds and Life Insurance (if applicable)

Add the number of stocks and bonds that the petitioner owns. The petitioner must list the stocks and bonds on the "Additional Information" sheet or on a separate document. List the serial numbers and denominations of the bonds and name of record owner(s). Provide the sum of the petitioner's life insurance and the cash surrender value.

Real Estate Information (if applicable)

Add the petitioner's real estate information. Add the value of all real estate owned, the mortgages, and debts. Add the location of the real estate. If there is more than one property, add them to "Additional Information" or attach a separate sheet of paper. On the separate sheet of paper type or print the petitioner's name and A-Number (if any) at the top of each sheet, indicate the Page Number and Item Number to which the answer refers, and sign and date each sheet.

Petitioner's Dependent Information (if applicable)

Provide the information of all people currently financially dependent on the petitioner (*NOTE: this should **not** include the foreign fiancé(e) who was already put into Part 2*). For example, if the petitioner has children or parents that they are financially responsible for, then add their full name, date of birth, and relationship to the petitioner. Indicate whether this person is wholly or partially dependent on the petitioner for support. Form I-134 has multiple entries for possible dependents, but if more entries are needed the petitioner can use "Additional Information" or a separate sheet of paper.

Part 4. Sponsor's Statement, Contact Information, Certification and Signature (I-134)

This is the final section for the petitioner and/or co-sponsor to certify that all the information in Form I-134, Affidavit of Support is authorized, complete, true, and correct.

The petitioner/sponsor or co-sponsor must indicate whether they can read and understand English. If not, there may be a need for an interpreter or preparer in Part 5 and Part 6. The sponsor/co-sponsor provide their telephone number and email (if any).

The sponsor/co-sponsor's signature confirms that everything in the document is authorized, complete, true, and correct.

Part 5. The Petitioner Used an Interpreter (I-134)

If the petitioner used anyone as an interpreter to read the instructions and questions on this affidavit in a language in which they are fluent, the interpreter must fill out this section, provide his or her name, the name and address of his or her business or organization (if any), his or her daytime telephone number, his or her mobile telephone number (if any), and his or her email address (if any). The interpreter must sign and date the affidavit.

Part 6. If Someone Else is Preparing the Document (if other than sponsor or co-sponsor) (I-134)

This part is for contact information, statement, declaration, and signature of the person preparing this Affidavit, if other than the sponsor or co-sponsor. This section must contain the signature of the person who completed your affidavit, if other than the sponsor. If the same individual acted as the interpreter and the preparer, that person should complete both Part 5 and Part 6. If the person who completed this affidavit is associated with a business or organization, that person should complete the business or organization name and address information. Anyone who helped complete this affidavit MUST sign and date the affidavit. A stamped or typewritten name in place of a signature is not acceptable. If the person who helped prepare the affidavit is an attorney or accredited representative whose representation extends beyond the preparation of this affidavit, he or she may be obliged to also submit a completed Form G-28, Notice of Entry of Appearance as Attorney or Accredited Representative, along with the affidavit.

The I-134, Affidavit of Support Re-Cap

A completed I-134, Affidavit of Support with an original signature will be useful to the consular officer to evaluate the petitioner's ability to financially support the foreign fiancé(e) when they get to the USA. The foreign fiancé(e) will need to have the petitioner's most recent U.S. Federal Income Tax Return (Form 1040) and wage statements (form W-2 or 1099). Unless otherwise stated by the embassy, the petitioner should include employment letters stating the salaries and bank statements as evidence backing up what is filled out on the I-134, affidavit of support. Click the link for I-134 information. http://www.uscis.gov/i-134.
See poverty guideline for income. http://aspe.hhs.gov

Step 3.7 – Embassy Preparation – Termination of Previous Marriage

If the foreign fiancé(e) or the U.S. petitioner have been married in the past, then they MUST provide evidence that any previous marriage(s) has ended. This evidence needs to be a copy of documents showing termination of a prior marriage. This could include official documents such as:

- divorce decree
- annulment decree
- death certificate

This will be an official document from a local government agency that proves ALL prior marriages contracted by the foreign fiancé(e) and the petitioner have been legally terminated prior to the filing of the petition. These documents must be brought to the U.S. embassy by the foreign fiancé(e).

People often ask if they need to include previous marriages from 20 – 30 years ago. The answer is YES. It doesn't matter how long ago the marriages were, the U.S. embassy can find old marriages very easily so it's best to be upfront and show evidence of those marriages being terminated.

If the I-129F was filed without identifying all terminated marriages and providing evidence, then this may result in NO visa. Usually, if there was a previous marriage, the U.S. embassy will ask for evidence of termination of marriage if it is not in the package provided.

Step 3.8 – Embassy Preparation – Pay and Schedule Visa Appointment

In this step, the U.S. petitioner and foreign fiancé(e) will be able to make a schedule and pay for the visa appointment.

The foreign fiancé(e) will receive instructions from the embassy on what to do. The instructions in this book are to give an idea of how it typically works but does not reflect what EVERY embassy requires. It is important to keep in mind that the foreign fiancé(e) will have to coordinate the medical appointment before they go to the U.S. embassy.

Paying for the visa fee & scheduling the appointment is slightly different from country to country. You can find this information on the following sites:

- http://www.ustraveldocs.com/
- https://ais.usvisa-info.com/
- https://travel.state.gov/content/travel/en/us-visas/visa-information-resources/list-of-posts.html
- Embassy site:
  - https://www.usembassy.gov

Since even some of the site information on official government sites can be inaccurate, it is best to CALL the embassy directly.

EXAMPLE of the VISA PAY and SCHEDULE Walkthrough

The following is an example of what must be done to schedule and pay for the visa appointment.   Please note that this process varies from country to country.

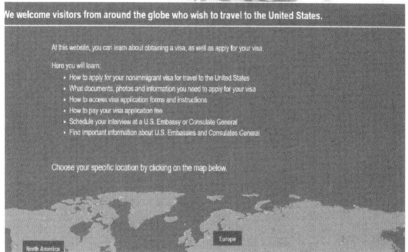

Go to www.ustraveldocs.com
At this website, the foreign fiancé(e) can learn about obtaining a visa, as well as apply for a visa. Here they can learn:

- How to apply for nonimmigrant visa for travel to the United States
- What documents, photos, and information are needed to apply for a visa
- How to access visa application forms and instructions
- How to pay the visa application fee
- Schedule an interview at a U.S. embassy or consulate general
- Find important information about U.S. embassies and consulates general

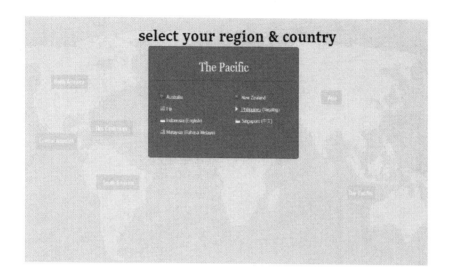

Select the region and the country that the foreign fiancé(e) will process their visa. If the foreign fiancé(e) is working abroad and not going back to their home country, they will need to go through the U.S. embassy in the country that they are currently in. The next step will be to select "nonimmigrant".

NOTE: AGAIN, how the visa interview is scheduled is different in each country. Once the foreign fiancé(e) clicks their country, how the visa fee is paid, and how the visa is scheduled will be different from country to country. So, the step-by-step screenshots will not apply to everyone. Some embassies have their own sites and portals that guide the foreign fiancé(e) through the process. For any questions, the best resource is always the embassy where the foreign fiancé(e) will have the interview.

#YuriBruce: Visa Approved series

Is this your first time applying for a visa and/or visiting our site?

Choose "YES". If you choose "NO", the site will take you to the front page which offers other services.

Select "Nonimmigrant" for the K-1 Visa.

Later in the process, the government will sometimes put K-1 under an "Immigrant" type visa because the purpose of K-1 is to allow the foreign fiancé(e) to become an immigrant after becoming a spouse and adjusting their status from nonimmigrant to immigrant.

Check out the Visa Fees.

The foreign fiancé(e) / U.S. petitioner will have to pay for the K-1 visa application. Ustraveldocs.com has information on how to pay the visa fee. The visa application fee amount is determined by the type of visa which is displayed on the visa fee page.

Visa Types and Application Fee Amounts - Sorted by Visa Type			
Visa Type	Description	Fee Amount (USD)	Fee Amount (PHP)
B	Business/Tourist	$160	8480.00
C-1	Transit	$160	8480.00
CW	Transitional Worker CNMI	$190	10070.00
D	Ship/Airline Crew	$160	8480.00
E	Treaty Trader/Investor, Australian Professional Specialty	$205	10865.00
F	Student (academic)	$160	8480.00
H	Temporary/Seasonal Workers and Employment, Trainees	$190	10070.00
I	Journalist and Media	$160	8480.00
J	Exchange Visitor	$160	8480.00
K	Fiancé(e) or Spouse of U.S. Citizen	$265	14045.00
L	Intracompany Transferees	$190	10070.00
M	Student (vocational)	$160	8480.00
O	Persons with Extraordinary Ability	$190	10070.00
P	Athletes, Artists & Entertainers	$190	10070.00
Q	International Cultural Exchange	$190	10070.00
R	Religious Worker	$190	10070.00
T	Victim of Human Trafficking	$160	8480.00
TN/TD	NAFTA Professionals	$160	8480.00
U	Victim of Criminal Activity	$160	8480.00

Visa Types and Application Fee Amounts are sorted by Visa Type. In the Philippines sample case, the fee is $265 USD (as of 2018). Each country has the same visa fee for K-1. The fee amount is displayed in the local currency and USD.

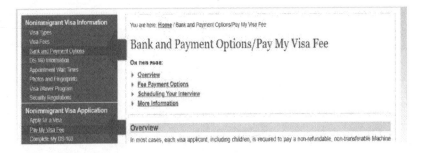

Go to Pay My Visa Fee OR Bank and Payment Options. This page will give instructions on how to pay the visa application fee

DO NOT print multiple copies of the same deposit slip. You must have a unique deposit slip for each transaction.

If you print a deposit slip in advance of the day in which you plan to make your payment, please take note of the expiration date on the deposit slip. If the expiration date passes prior to using the slip to make your payment, simply return to this site and re-click the appropriate link below to generate a new deposit slip. Bank agents will NOT accept payments based on expired deposit slips. Upon receiving of your payment, bank will issue you a receipt. Save your receipt. It cannot be replaced if it is lost. You will not be able to schedule an appointment without your receipt number.

Select the deposit slip that matches your visa application fee from the list below. Values are shown in U.S. dollars and native currency. This page has more information about the different visa application fees.

‣ Deposit Slip - $160 MRV Fee
‣ Deposit Slip - $190 MRV Fee
‣ Deposit Slip - $265 MRV Fee
‣ Deposit Slip - $205 MRV Fee

After you have paid the visa application fee, keep the BANK receipt for your records. It cannot be replaced if it is lost. You will not be able to schedule an appointment without your receipt number.

Online Payment

If you have an account with either Bank of Philippine Islands (BPI) or BancNet you may choose to pay your visa application fee online using their online bill pay services. Click on either of the links below if you are a BPI or BancNet customer and wish to make an online payment.

‣ BPI
‣ Bancnet

Fee Payment Options Are different in Every Country. In this example, for the Philippines, the visa fee is $265 USD (as of 2018). The Philippines allows the applicant to pay for the nonimmigrant visa application fee with cash at any Bank of Philippine Islands. Before going to the bank, you must print the applicable U.S. visa application deposit slip available (Figure, Visa Fee Deposit Slip) on this page. Take the printed deposit slip to pay your fee.

Figure, Visa Fee Deposit Slip

U.S. Visa Fee Deposit Slip, Receipt and Receipt Number.
The Philippines sample includes a receipt and receipt number that will be important to fill out the visa schedule.

Schedule Appointments.
Each country has different rules and processes for scheduling appointments. The U.S. embassy where the foreign fiancé(e) is going through is supposed to send information about the process.

▶ Your visa application (MRV) fee payment receipt
▶ Your DS-160 confirmation page
▶ Your e-mail address
▶ If applicable, required documents based on visa class (such as a petition approval for petition-based visas; more information about visa types and information about each can be found here).

Restrictions to Changing Appointments

Please be reminded that even though nonimmigrant visa fees are valid for one calendar year, options to schedule an appointment are limited. The U.S. Embassy in Manila schedules hundreds of thousands of nonimmigrant visa appointments each year and must accommodate requests both for new appointments and for those applicants who need to reschedule their appointments for whatever reason. Applicants are only allowed to reschedule twice (not including the initial appointment) without penalty. If the second rescheduling attempt is canceled, an applicant will only be allowed to reschedule a new date after a waiting period of 90 days. Please plan your visa application accordingly to avoid problems securing an interview appointment.

More Actions

Schedule an appointment
Change your appointment

Schedule or Change an Appointment. At the bottom of the *"Schedule My Appointment"* page, there is a link under "More Actions" that allows the applicant to schedule or change an appointment.

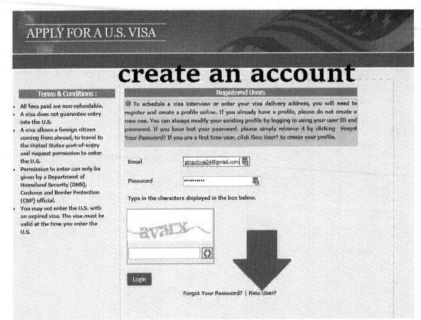

Create a User Account on **https://cgifederal.secure.force.com** after being forwarded from ustraveldocs.com and sign in.

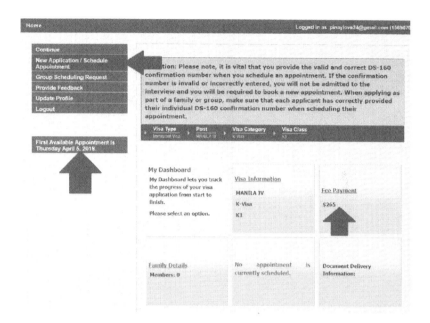

New Application / Schedule Appointment. The "New Application" page will display the first available appointment. Make sure the foreign fiancé(e) has enough time to complete the medical appointment before the embassy interview. The medical exam takes 1 day to do. The medical facility will let the foreign fiancé know when the results will be ready to be sent to the U.S. embassy.

Also, ensure the foreign fiancé(e) provides valid and correct DS-160 confirmation number when scheduling an appointment. If the confirmation number is invalid or incorrectly entered, they may not be admitted to the interview and will be required to book a new appointment. When applying as part of a family or group, make sure that each applicant has correctly provided their individual DS-160 confirmation number when scheduling their appointment.

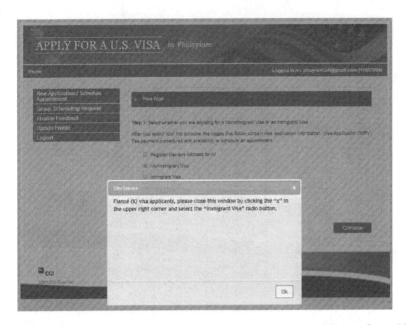

Visa Type - Don't Use Nonimmigrant Visa for K-1. If "Nonimmigrant Visa" is selected, the applicant will get the following message box:

"Fiancé (K) visa applicants, please close this window by clicking the "x" in the upper right corner and select the "Immigrant Visa" radio button."

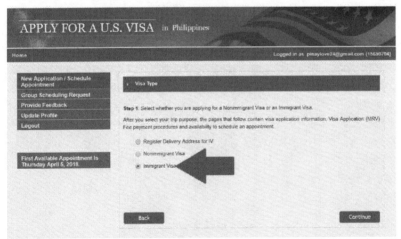

Visa Type - Immigrant Visa. In this case, the K-1 is categorized as an immigrant visa.

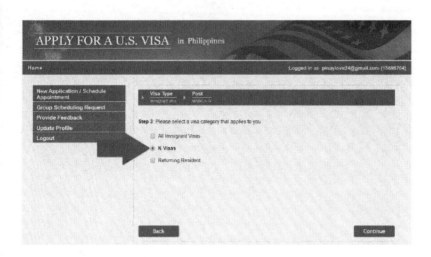

Select K Visas. K-1 is among other "K" visas.

K-1 - Fiancé(e) of U.S. Citizen. Select K-1 and it will allow the applicant to add a K-2 (child of a foreign fiancé(e)) later.

#YuriBruce: Visa Approved series

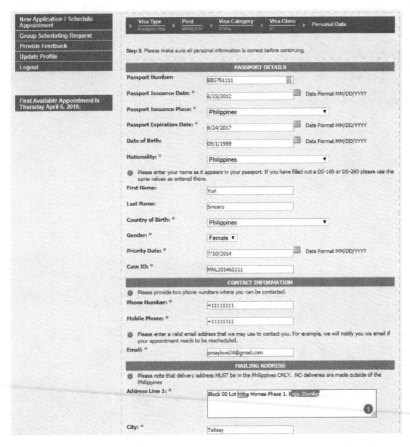

New Application / Schedule Appointment. Put in passport details, contact information, and mailing address.

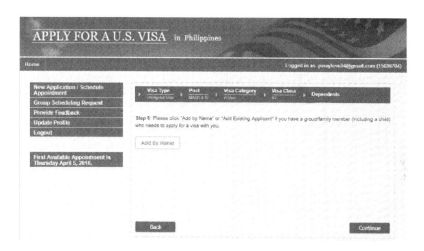

Add by Name (K-2). In order to add a child, K-2, click "Add by Name". A child (unmarried and under 21 years of age) of a K-1 or K-3 nonimmigrant may apply for a nonimmigrant visa to accompany or follow-to-join the K-1 or K-3 parent. The applicant does not need to file a separate petition to classify the child as a K nonimmigrant. Children of K-1s are classified as K-2 nonimmigrants, and children of K-3s are classified as K-4 nonimmigrants.

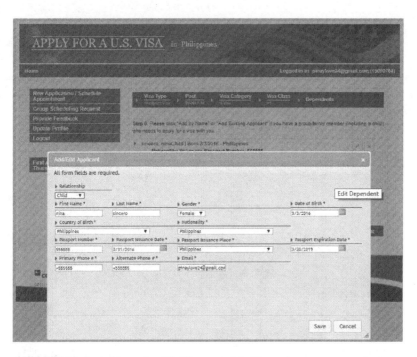

Add/Edit Applicant (K-2). Add the name, gender, country, and the nationality of the K-2.

Specify Documentation Delivery (visa address). If the foreign fiancé(e) selects "Home Delivery" or "Office Delivery", make sure this address is accurate. This is where the visa will be delivered.

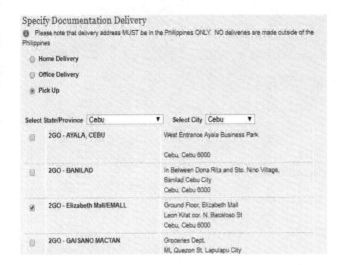

If the foreign fiancé(e) selects "Pick Up", then they will have to select the "state/province", "state" and the address of the nearest pickup location will appear on the screen.

Enter Visa Receipt Information. In the Philippines sample, the applicant should have an MRV receipt Number for the K-1 foreign fiancé(e) and the K-2 child of the foreign fiancé(e) (if any).

Enter Visa Receipt Information. In the Philippines sample, the applicant should have an MRV receipt Number for the K-1 foreign fiancé(e) and the K-2 child of the foreign fiancé(e) (if any).

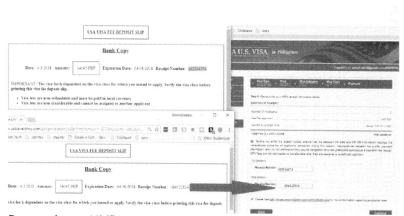

Put the MVR receipt number in the "Schedule My Appointment" Page

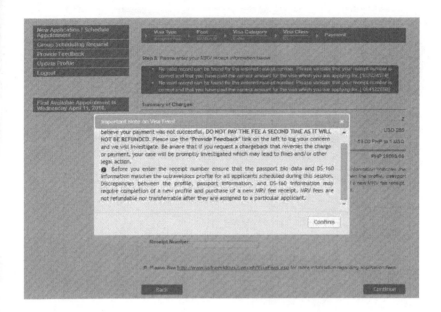

Visa Fees are not refundable. If you have encountered an error with your payment or you believe your payment was not successful, DO NOT PAY THE FEE A SECOND TIME AS IT WILL NOT BE REFUNDED. Please use the "Provide Feedback" link on the left to log your concern and we will investigate. Be aware that if you request a chargeback that reverses the charge or payment, your case will be promptly investigated which may lead to fines and/or other legal action.

Before you enter the receipt number, ensure that the passport biographic data and DS-160 information matches the ustraveldocs profile for all applicants scheduled during this session. Discrepancies between the profile, passport information, and DS-160 information may require completion of a new profile and purchase of a new MRV fee receipt. MRV fees are not refundable nor transferable after they are assigned to an applicant.

Schedule Consular Appointment. The schedule consular appointment page allows the foreign fiancé(e) to schedule the day that they will go to the appointment. It is VERY important to coordinate the medical exam with the embassy interview because of the medical results must be available for the embassy interview.

Step 3. References:

"I-129F, Petition for Alien Fiancé(e)." USCIS, 5 May 2018, https://www.uscis.gov/i-129f

"National Visa Center." U.S. Department of State - Bureau of Consular Affairs, 9 May 2018, https://travel.state.gov/content/travel/en/us-visas/immigrate/national-visa-center.html

"NVC Contact Information." U.S. Department of State - Bureau of Consular Affairs, 9 May 2018, https://travel.state.gov/content/travel/en/us-visas/immigrate/national-visa-center/nvc-contact-information.html

"Form I-129F Instructions." USCIS, 5 May 2018, https://www.uscis.gov/sites/default/files/files/form/i-129finstr.pdf

"DS-160, Online Nonimmigrant Visa Application." U.S. Department of State - Bureau of Consular Affairs, 9 May 2018, https://ceac.state.gov/genniv/

"Form I-134 Instructions." USCIS, 10 May 2018, https://www.uscis.gov/sites/default/files/files/form/i-134instr.pdf

"Form I-134, Affidavit of Support." USCIS, 5 May 2018, https://www.uscis.gov/i-134

"Form I-797: Types and Functions." USCIS, 5 May 2018, https://www.uscis.gov/i-797-info

"Poverty Guidelines." Office of The Assistant Secretary for Planning and Evaluation (ASPE), 5 May 2018, https://aspe.hhs.gov/poverty-guidelines

"What is the difference between an Immigrant Visa vs. Nonimmigrant Visa?" U.S. Customs and Border Protection, 5 May 2018, https://help.cbp.gov/app/answers/detail/a_id/72/~/what-is-the-difference-between-an-immigrant-visa-vs.-nonimmigrant-visa-%3F

"Nonimmigrant Visa for a Fiancé (K-1)." U.S. Department of State - Bureau of Consular Affairs, 9 May 2018 https://travel.state.gov/content/travel/en/us-visas/immigrate/family-immigration/nonimmigrant-visa-for-a-fiance-k-1.htm

"Apply for A U.S. Visa." U.S. Department of State - Bureau of Consular Affairs, 9 May 2018, https://www.ustraveldocs.com

Step 4. Medical
Step 4.0 - Medical Overview

The foreign fiancé(e) and children are required to go through a medical exam with a U.S. immigration approved facility or physician. The results of the medical exam become part of the U.S. embassy interview, so the exam must be conducted prior to the interview.

We will talk about what goes on in the medical exam, what they are looking for, and how to prepare.

Before Medical Exam Checklist

Before Medical Exam Checklist	
Tasks/Documents	
U.S. Embassy Instruction for U.S. Immigration Approved Medical Exam. The U.S. embassy will give the foreign fiancé(e) instructions which include the eligibility letter. The instructions will explain where to go and what is needed for the medical exam. Even with resources online, the foreign fiancé(e) should make sure that the medical facility or physician they found is where the U.S. embassy directs them to go.	
Visa Interview Appointment Letter. The medical facility or physician will ask for a Visa Interview Confirmation form from the U.S. Embassy. The foreign fiancé can also bring a copy of the online registration confirmation form.	
Passport. The foreign fiancé(e) needs a current passport.	
Photocopy of the Passport (if required by medical facility). In the case of the U.S. Embassy in Manila, they require a photocopy of the Passport biographic page. The page in the passport that contains the applicant's photo and information.	

Figure, Step 4 Checklist (part 1)

#YuriBruce: Visa Approved series

The U.S. embassy is supposed to mail the foreign fiancé a letter with detailed instructions on where to go and what to do for the medical exam.

(4) Passport Style Photos. The number of passport-style photos may vary.	
Immunization / Medical Records (if applicable). The foreign fiancé(e) will receive instructions on whether or not they need immunization / medical records.	
Letter with Case Number (if required by medical facility). Some medical facilities will ask for a letter with the case number. An example of this would be the DS-160 confirmation page.	

#YuriBruce: Visa Approved series

Embassy of the United States of America

Manila, Philippines

Date : 10 Jun 2014

YURI MAHINAY SINCERO
BLK 11 LOT 29 MINGLANILLA PHASE
BRGY. OPRA CEBU 6000 CEBU

PHILIPPINES

SLMCEC-POS

Dear SINCERO, YURI MAHINAY:

This refers to your fiancé(e) (K1/K3) visa case.

Your case is eligible to be scheduled for a visa interview. You must pay the K visa application fee before you can schedule a visa appointment.

To schedule a visa interview appointment, please visit this website: http://www.ustraveldocs.com or call the Visa Information and Appointment Service at (632)-982-5555 or (632) 902-8930. Callers in the USA may contact the Appointment Service at (214) 571-1600. The Call Center is open Monday through Friday, from 8:00 a.m. to 8:00 p.m. (Manila time), except on U.S. and Philippine holidays. You must have the case number, passport number, and passport expiry date for each applicant (principal applicant and derivative family members) ready when requesting a visa appointment.

If you are unable to keep your visa appointment date, please visit the same website or call the Visa Information and Appointment Service to reschedule your visa appointment.

IMPORTANT INFORMATION

Please read and follow all application and interview preparation instructions for fiancé(e) K1/K3 visa applicants located on the Embassy's web site at http://manila.usembassy.gov/wwwh3279.html The instructions contained at the web site will inform you of the required documentation and procedures to follow prior to the interview date. All K1/K3 applicants are required to complete form DS-160 and print the confirmation page to be presented at the time of interview. Any K applicant without completed application forms who appears for an interview will be referred to nearby internet cafés to complete the application forms. Applicants who can complete the forms and return to the Embassy by 10:00 am will still be interviewed on the same day. Applicants who cannot or choose not to return to the Embassy with the completed forms by 10:00 am will be advised to reschedule the interview by visiting the online appointment website at http://www.ustraveldocs.com/ph or by calling the Call Center at (632) 982-5555 or (632) 902-8930.

Enclosed please find material explaining the Legal Rights Available to Immigrant Victims of Domestic Violence in the United States. For more information, visit the USCIS website at: http://tinyurl.com/USCIS-info

When communicating with the Embassy by telephone, e-mail, letter, or fax, always   refer to your name, case number and visa category as they appear below.

Sincerely,

Chief, Immigrant Visa Branch

Case Number : MNL20142346486
Name (P) : SINCERO, YURI MAHINAY

Traveling Applicants :
(P) SINCERO, YURI MAHINAY   02 MAR 1988

Figure, Embassy Case Eligibility Letter

Step 4.1 - U.S. Embassy Medical Instructions

Before the foreign fiancé(e) goes to the U.S. embassy interview they must have a medical exam at a U.S. immigration approved clinic or physician. This means that they need to coordinate the date of the medical exam results with the schedule of the U.S. embassy Interview. The medical process at each immigration approved clinic in each country is different, so make sure the foreign fiancé(e) reads the instructions and double checks with the U.S. embassy they will be going to. If the foreign fiancé(e) does not have the medical exam results before they go to the U.S. embassy interview, it will delay the visa case until the U.S. embassy can get those results. The foreign fiancé(e) may need to reschedule the interview until the medical results are released.

Finding the Embassy Approved Medical Facility

The First Step in preparing for the medical examination is to determine which doctor or medical facilities in the foreign fiancé(e)'s area is authorized to perform a medical examination for U.S. immigration. They cannot go to just any medical clinic. It must be one authorized by U.S. immigration.

The embassy should send the foreign fiancé(e) a visa letter that will list authorized physicians or medical facilities. This will include instructions on what is required, how much it costs, and where to pay for the medical exam. The foreign fiancé(e) or the U.S. petitioner should contact the U.S. embassy via phone and email if the instructions are not received after 30 days of the I-129F case getting to the U.S. embassy. The embassy will have resources and information to give.

Medical Resources

The State Department has a list of places on their site but make sure to double check these and their instructions because they do change them from time to time. Check this list of embassies and consulates to get specific instructions (this list is broken down by the city that the embassy/consulate is in):

- https://travel.state.gov/content/travel/en/us-visas/visa-information-resources/list-of-posts.html

NOTE: The embassies and consulates change processes and procedures often, so make sure the petitioner or foreign fiancé(e) contacts the applicable embassy/consulate to double check what is needed for medical and where to go.

Medical Examinations Differ Per Country

Medical examinations for U.S. immigration are different for each country. The prices of the procedure, time frame, and requirements are different because there are different currencies, different customs, and different laws.

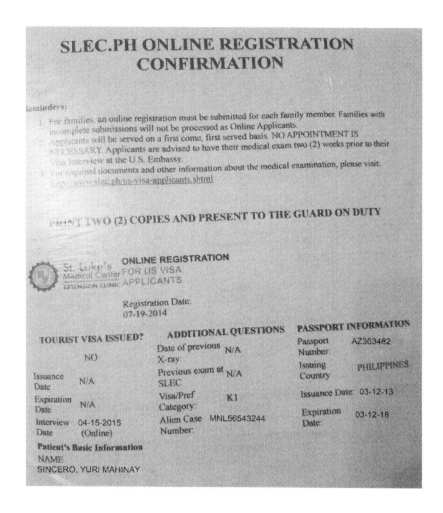

Figure, St. Luke's Medical Center in Manila

Each medical center and physician does things a little differently as far as managing people coming in and out.

Here are some examples:

In Abu Dhabi, United Arab Emirates, they want the foreign fiancé(e) to bring the following requirements (as of 2018):

- Visa interview appointment letter
- Foreign fiancé(e)'s passport
- Four (4) recently taken passport-sized color photographs

- A copy of your immunization records
- More   information: https://travel.state.gov/content/dam/visas/iv-dv-supplemental/ABD_Abu-Dhabi.pdf

Accra, Ghana, is different from Abu Dhabi but has similarities. They state that the foreign fiancé(e) should allow 14 days to complete the medical examination process from start to finish. The foreign fiancé(e) must bring the following (as of 2018):

- Visa interview appointment letter
- Foreign fiancé(e)'s passport
- Three (3) recently taken passport-sized color photographs
- A copy of your immunization records
- More information: *https://travel.state.gov/content/dam/visas/iv-dv-supplemental/ACC_Accra.pdf*

Cairo, Egypt requires that the foreign fiancé(e) brings the following:

- Visa interview appointment letter
- Foreign fiancé(e)'s passport
- Three (3) recently taken passport-sized color photographs
- A copy of your immunization records
- Medical records including prescription information, for any medical conditions you currently have

Manila, Philippines requires that the following be brought to the examination:

- Visa interview appointment letter
- Letter with the case number (NVC or Eligibility letter)
- Foreign fiancé(e)'s passport & 1 photocopy
- Three (3) recently taken passport-sized color photographs
- A copy of your immunization records

NOTE: The embassy process is subject to frequent change - contact the embassy/consulate to verify the document released.

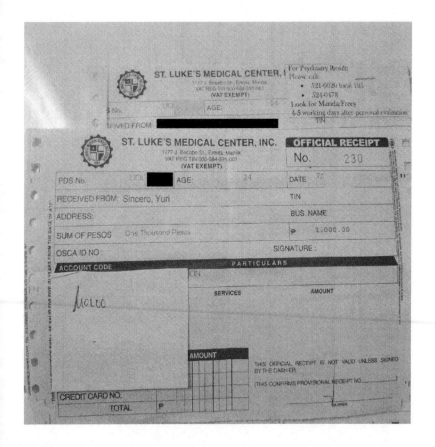

Figure, St. Luke's Medical Receipt

Each medical center in each country will offer different methods of payment. The price varies.

What to Expect in the Medical Exam

What is the foreign fiancé(e) going to experience during the medical exam?
The medical examination will include a medical history review, physical examination, and chest X-ray, gonorrhea test, and blood tests (for applicants 15 years of age or older). The United States also requires tuberculosis (TB) testing for all applicants two years of age and older. The foreign fiancé(e) should be prepared to discuss their medical history, medications they are taking, and current treatments they are undergoing.

U.S. immigration law requires immigrant visa applicants to obtain certain vaccinations prior to the issuance of a visa. For more information about the shots and why they give them, you can check out CDC.GOV page on immigration vaccinations.

- **https://www.cdc.gov/immigrantrefugeehealth/exams/ ti/panel/vaccination-panel-technical-instructions.html**

Can Medical Conditions Stop the Foreign Fiancé(e) From Entering the USA?

We have talked to people diagnosed with cancer and other diseases that have gotten through the process and into the USA with no problems.

There are some communicable diseases that will delay the foreign fiancé(e) from getting the K-1 visa. The Department of Health and Human Services (HHS) have identified the following "communicable diseases of public health significance" for the immigration medical examinations to look for:

- •Gonorrhea;
- •Leprosy, infectious;
- •Syphilis, infectious stage; and
- •Tuberculosis (TB), Active—Only a Class A TB diagnosis renders an applicant inadmissible to the United States.

These are treatable diseases. People with these diseases will have to undergo treatment before getting the visa. Although treatment can take months, U.S. immigration will not deny the applicant once the disease is no longer communicable.

Human Immunodeficiency Virus (HIV)

Human immunodeficiency virus (HIV) infection is no longer categorized as a communicable disease of public health significance according to HHS regulations. An HIV diagnosis will not stop a foreign fiancé(e) from getting a visa. This changed back in January 2010.

NOTE: Herpes is also not categorized as a "communicable disease of public health significance" either.

Mental Disorders & Drug Abuse

If the foreign fiancé(e) admits to drug use or if the medical screeners determine that the foreign fiancé(e) has a mental disorder, they may recommend additional screening with a mental health care professional. It is best to be truthful. The U.S. immigration medical examiner is looking for mental disorders that are associated with harmful behaviors or substance-abuse (drug addicts).

According to the Immigration and Nationality Act, there are three grounds of inadmissibility related to drug addiction, or mental disorders that affect behavior:

- Current physical or mental disorder with associated harmful behavior.
- Past physical or mental disorder with associated harmful behavior, if the harmful behavior is likely to recur or lead to other harmful behavior in the future.
- Drug (substance) abuse or addiction (medically called dependence). Dependence on or abuse of any of the substances listed in Section 202 of the Controlled Substances Act (Appendix C).

Medical Results

How medical results are handled will vary depending on the country. In some cases, the U.S. embassy receives the medical results directly from the medical facility. But sometimes the medical results are given to the foreign fiancé(e) to be taken to the U.S. embassy. The foreign fiancé(e) will be instructed on exactly what to do. In this case, after the medical exam, the doctor will provide the foreign fiancé(e) with exam results in a sealed envelope. DO NOT OPEN THIS ENVELOPE. Instead, bring it to the U.S. embassy interview. Any x-rays taken may also be given to the foreign fiancé(e).

Step 4. References:

"Center for Disease Control and Prevention." CDC, 10 May 2018,
https://www.cdc.gov/immigrantrefugeehealth/exams/ti/panel/mental-panel-technical-instructions.htm

"Center for Disease Control and Prevention." CDC, 11 May 2018,
https://www.cdc.gov/immigrantrefugeehealth/laws-regulations.html

"Title 21 USC Controlled Substance Act." USDOJ.gov, 10 May 2018,
https://www.deadiversion.usdoj.gov/21cfr/21usc/812.htm

"Chapter 6 - Communicable Diseases of Public Health Significance." USCIS, 11 May 2018,
https://www.uscis.gov/policymanual/HTML/PolicyManual-Volume8-PartB-Chapter6.html

"Nonimmigrant Visa for a Fianc(é)e (K-1)." U.S. Department of State - Bureau of Consular Affairs, 9 May 2018
https://travel.state.gov/content/travel/en/us-visas/immigrate/family-immigration/nonimmigrant-visa-for-a-fiance-k-1.htm

"Apply for A U.S. Visa." U.S. Department of State - Bureau of Consular Affairs, 9 May 2018,
https://www.ustraveldocs.com

Step 5. Interview
Step 5.0 - Interview Overview

By this time, the U.S. petitioner has gotten the I-129F approved. The petitioner and the foreign fiancé(e) have the case number and the I-129F is at the U.S. embassy. The foreign fiancé(e) has all necessary documents and has completed the medical exam. The foreign fiancé(e) should also have a scheduled interview with the U.S. embassy.
In this step, we are going to review everything the foreign fiancé(e) should have before they go to the Interview. We are going to go through the types of questions they ask, types of consular officers, and how to prepare for the interview.
U.S. petitioner does not need to attend the interview, but they can at certain embassies. The focus of the interview will be on the foreign fiancé(e) and the relationship.

Interview Checklist

Interview Checklist	
Tasks/Documents	
Open Communication with Fiancé(e). Make sure you and your fiancé(e) have a legit relationship. You should know each other's personal history and talk openly and honestly about what happened with past marriages and criminal history. The consular officer may ask about these things in the interview.	
Review Embassy Checklist. Double check all required documents detailed in the "Embassy Checklist" in this book. Have all these documents in an easily accessible, organized book, binder, or folder that can be carried into the U.S. embassy.	

Interview Checklist (continued)

Have a Copy of Nonimmigrant Visa Electronic Confirmation Page (DS-160). Print the DS-160 Confirmation Page that contains the barcode information to bring to your interview. This is needed to get into the U.S. embassy. https://ceac.state.gov/genniv/	
Medical Results from Medical Examination. All K-1 and K-2 visa applicants must complete a medical examination at a U.S. immigration approved physician or facility. Medical results will be given to the U.S. embassy directly or delivered by the foreign fiancé(e) during the interview.	
Passport. The foreign fiancé(e) must have a passport that is valid for at least 6 months at the time of the interview.	
Practice the Potential Questions. In this book, there are potential questions that the consular officer may ask. Go through all the questions and practice the responses.	
DO NOT BRING ELECTRONICS INTO THE EMBASSY. Do not bring any electronic devices such as phones, headphones, tablets, including USB, in your interview. Applicants who bring devices will be denied entry into the building or be required to leave them outside the facility.	

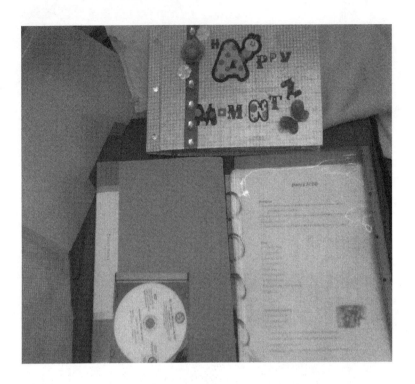

Figure, Example of embassy interview documents (booklets)

This package includes a book of pictures of the couple together, I-134, and other required documents.

Step 5.1 - What is the U.S. Embassy Like?

U.S. embassies have security similar to airports with the seriousness of a military base. There are often security checkpoints outside with armed guards and security cameras. Before coming inside, the foreign fiancé(e) must have an appointment that is confirmed with the DS-160 confirmation page. Before going into the main portion of the building, everyone must go through a metal detector. Phones, USBs, laptops, cameras are not allowed inside the embassy.

Figure, Manila Embassy courtyard waiting area

Applicants are sent outside to wait to be called. They need a lot of chairs because there are 100's of people to process.

Some embassies are very busy because they are processing many kinds of visas and interacting with 100's of people per day. So, the lines may be long and it may take hours to be seen. It is best not to schedule anything else for the day because getting the interview could take most of the day.

Figure, Manila U.S. Embassy consular officer window booths
Inside of this embassy, the applicants do not go into an office. They are interviewed at window booths

What is the Interview Like?

The interview experience itself will vary from case to case and from consular officer to consular officer. Some consular officers will be asking lots of questions and be very critical and others will ask very few questions. We have heard of interviews lasting up to an hour and some lasting a few minutes. The experience is much easier for the foreign fiancé(e) if they are prepared. Things they can do to prepare include:

- Double check all the required documents
- Write down possible questions
- Practice all possible questions with the fiancé(e)
- Ask others about their experience with the interview
- Visualize doing very well in the interview

During the interview process, the embassy will take the foreign fiancé(e)'s documents. They also take the passport which will be returned after the final decision is made. The passport may be delivered to the applicant's home, office, or at embassy designated organizations. This depends on the applicant's request and what country they are in.

Step 5.2 - Interview Questions

We noticed that foreign fiancé(e)s are most nervous about the interview. But it usually turns out to be one of the easiest parts of the entire process. Success favors the prepared! The interview is subjective, meaning sometimes the consular officer asks a lot of questions and sometimes they don't. If the foreign fiancé(e) comes unprepared then there is a chance that the consular officer will ask more and more questions. If the foreign fiancé(e) is prepared (has all documents, has talked to the U.S. petitioner about the relationship and previous marriages, has reviewed possible questions), then no matter how much they ask, the foreign fiancé(e) is ready.

We've broken the questions into categories to give an idea of where they focus and to help the foreign fiancé(e) prepare:

1. Basic information about the foreign fiancé(e) / petitioner
2. Petitioner and foreign fiancé(e) relationship
3. U.S. petitioner's job and finances
4. Previous Marriages
5. Criminal history

1. **Basic information**
   a. Things like you and your fiancé(e)'s FULL Name, DOB, where they live
   b. Sample questions include:
      i. What is your name?
      ii. What is your petitioner's name?
      iii. What is your relation to the petitioner?
      iv. When is your petitioner's birthday?
      v. When is your birthday?
      vi. Where was your fiancé(e) born?
      vii. Where does your fiancé(e) live?

2. **Petitioner   and   Foreign   Fiancé(e) Relationship**
   a. This includes: personal relationship, meeting each other, kids
   b. An example of these questions would be:
      i. How did you meet your fiancé(e)?
      ii.   When did you meet in person?
      iii.   How did he (or you) propose?
      iv.   Does the U.S. petitioner have kids?
      v.   What are the names of the kids? How old are they?
      vi.   How long have you been together?
      vii.   How many times did he visit you?

3. **U.S. Petitioner's Job and Finances**
   a. These are questions about your fiancé(e)'s income and financial situation
   b. Questions might include:
      i. What is your fiancé(e)'s living conditions, does he live in a house or apartment?
      ii.   Does your fiancé(e) have a house?
      iii.   Does your fiancé(e) live there?
      iv.   How much is his annual income?
      v.   What is their job or business?

4. **Previous Marriages**
   a. Questions might be:
      i. Do you know if your fiancé(e) was married before?

5. **Criminal History**
   a. If there is a criminal history for the fiancé(e) they might ask questions like:
      i. Do you know the fiancé's criminal history?

With these very personal types of questions, it is important for the petitioner and the foreign fiancé(e) to talk openly and honestly about everything from divorces to kids, to where they plan to live and finances. These are just some of the possible K-1 visa interview questions that may be asked.

The number of questions that they ask will vary. In Yuri's experience, she was asked 25 questions in 10 minutes. Preparation is the key to not missing anything that they ask.

Here are some sample questions gathered from foreign fiancé(e)s who were interviewed:

- What is your name?
- What is your petitioner's name?
- What is your relation to the petitioner?
- When is your petitioner's birthday?
- When is your birthday?
- Where was your fiancé(e) born?
- Where does your fiancé(e) live?
- What are his parents' names?
- What do they do for a living?
- Where do your fiancé(e)'s parents live?
- How did you meet your fiancé(e)?
- When did you meet in person?
- How did he (or you) propose?
- Have you ever been married before?
- Where did you first meet?
- How long have you been together?
- How many times did he visit you?

- How much time have you spent together?
- Where did the visit take place and when?
- When is the last time you have seen your fiancé(e)?
- Where did your fiancé(e) stay when he was visiting you?
- What can you say about your fiancé(e)?
- When will you leave for the US?
- What does your fiancé(e) like, coffee or tea?

- If married, do you have copies of your fiancé(e)'s divorce decree?

- How many times did he get divorced?
- What is the reason for his divorce?
- Does your fiancé(e) have any children? How many and how old are they? What are their names?
- When is/are their birthdays?
- Are you aware if he is paying alimony?
- Where do the kids live? With him or their mom?
- Are you aware of the kid's setup and their agreement? Do they live with your fiancé?
- What is your fiancé(e)'s living conditions, does he live in a house or apartment?
- Does your fiancé(e) have a house?
- Does your fiancé(e) live there?
- How much is his annual income?
- What does your fiancé(e) do for a living?
- How often do you communicate?
- What is the form of communication?
- Do you have your conversations, may I see?

- How many times have you traveled abroad? State the date and place of travel.
- Did you go there for work or vacation? And who was with you?
- Are you fully sure that you didn't go there for work?
- Are you aware of what you are going to do after arriving in the United States?
- Where are you getting married?
- When do you plan to get married?
- If your spouse cheats, what would you do?
- Are you planning to have children?
- Have you ever been to the US?
- Have you ever applied for a traveling visa?
- (If you have been to the U.S. before), what kind of visa did you travel in the US?
- Does your fiancé(e) have any brothers and sisters?
- Do you have brothers and sisters?
- Do you have other relatives living in the United States?
- Do you have your photos with you? Let me see them. (Put the dates and the locations of where the photos were taken.)
- How long have you been corresponding with your fiancé(e)?
- Do you know if your fiancé(e) was married before?
- What is your fiancé(e)'s religious background?
- Does your fiancé(e) speak and understand your language?
- Do you speak and understand your fiancé(e)'s language?

Interview Question Tips:

- Overcome nervousness with preparation
- Listen carefully to the questions
- Practice for days before the interview
- Do not keep changing your answers

Step 5. References:

"U.S. Visa Policy." U.S. Department of State - Bureau of Consular Affairs, 9 May 2018
https://travel.state.gov/content/travel/en/legal/visa-law0/laws-regulations/us-visa-policy.html
"Foreign Affairs Manual." U.S. Department of State - Bureau of Consular Affairs, 9 May 2018,
https://fam.state.gov/Fam/FAM.aspx
"Nonimmigrant Visa for a Fianc(é)e (K-1)." U.S. Department of State - Bureau of Consular Affairs, 9 May 2018
https://travel.state.gov/content/travel/en/us-visas/immigrate/family-immigration/nonimmigrant-visa-for-a-fiance-k-1.htm
"Apply for A U.S. Visa." U.S. Department of State - Bureau of Consular Affairs, 9 May 2018,
https://www.ustraveldocs.com

Visa Approved!

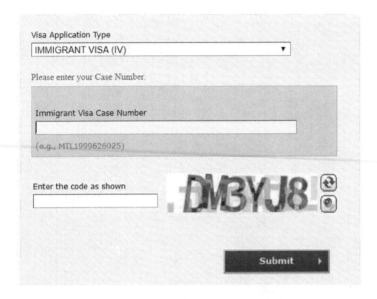

Figure, Visa Status Check

The consular officer sometimes tells the foreign fiancé(e) that they are approved on the spot with a "Welcome to America!" and other times they tell the foreign fiancé(e) to expect an answer within 1 - 2 weeks. The approval is announced via mail and on the site: (https://ceac.state.gov/ceac/).

Figure, K-1 Visa Within the Passport of the Foreign National

This is Yuri's K-1 visa in her passport. She got this back in 2014. The visa is a sticker with the foreign fiancé(e)'s passport style picture and information. It includes the date of issuance and expiration date.

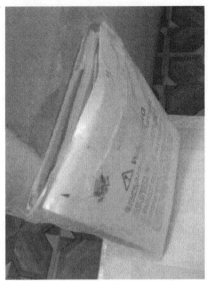

Figure, Packet from U.S. embassy

Once they have made a final decision and/or created the visa, the U.S. embassy will send the foreign fiancé(e) a packet with their passport and all the evidence that was submitted. They will also give instructions on what to do with the packet.

What If I Get a Visa Denial?

In some cases, the U.S. consular asks for additional information or flat out denies the visa. If they ask for additional information, this is done on a form called a 221g (based on the Immigration and Nationality Act section 221(g) due to failure to provide some information or document). The foreign fiancé(e) must comply with the U.S. embassy's request.

Figure, 221(g) Denial

If the consular officer doesn't feel that there is sufficient and consistent evidence of a real relationship, the consular officer will deny the visa stating, *"It was not established that the beneficiary and petitioner have a bona fide relationship."* The U.S. embassy sends the package back to the USCIS. The couple will be able to contact the USCIS once the package goes back. This takes a long time. From what we have seen, it takes months for the package to go back and it's better to just start the entire process over again. Other options may be to get an immigration lawyer, authorized service, or do a marriage visa instead.

Get the Green Card (BONUS Chapter)

Once the foreign fiancé(e) has the visa, they can get a plane ticket to the USA. The foreign fiancé(e) will give the embassy packet to immigration at the U.S. point of entry (POE). Some countries require the foreign fiancé(e) to go through a seminar prior to leaving. The Philippines, for example, has the Commission on Filipinos Overseas (CFO) which has a mandatory briefing on safety before Filipino fiancés travel overseas.

The foreign fiancé(e) and U.S. petitioner must get married within 90 days of arrival. After they are married, the foreign spouse can get their social security card and then file an I-485. The I-485 is the application to register permanent residence. This allows the foreign spouse to adjust their status from nonimmigrant to immigrant for a green card.

- https://www.uscis.gov/i-485

Once the I-485 is filed with the USCIS (and approved), the foreign spouse will get an appointment to have their biometrics collected by the U.S. government. This consists of fingerprints, height, weight, and basic information. Depending on the case and the state, the USCIS may ask for an interview before deciding whether or not the foreign spouse can have a permanent legal resident card (green card).

The timeframe of the green card varies from state to state. It can take anywhere from a few months to one year to get. If the foreign spouse files an I-765, Application for Employment Authorization and I-131, Application for Travel Document with the I-485, they will get an employment authorization document (EAD) combo card that comes within 2 - 4 months and allows them to work legally and come back into the USA if they travel to another country.

Figure, I-512 Advance Parole (EAD - Employment Authorization Document)
This card allows the foreign spouse to work and return to the U.S. if they leave for vacation or emergency.

2-Year Conditional Green Card

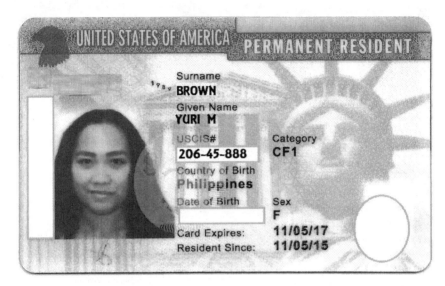

Figure, 2 Year Conditional Green Card

Upon approval of the I-485, the USCIS issues a green card that is good for two years. It is a conditional permanent residence that is issued based on evidence of a legitimate relationship at the time of marriage.

You and your spouse must apply together to remove the conditions on your residence by filing Form I-751. You must apply during the 90 days before your second anniversary as a conditional resident. The expiration date on your green card is also the date of your second anniversary as a conditional resident. If you do not apply to remove the conditions in time, you could lose your conditional resident status and be removed from the country.

Resources and Contacts

During our Fiancé(e) Visa to USA process, we used a LOT of resources. Some of these resources. Not all the resources we used are from the government. But the government resources are the most important.

U.S. Citizenship and Immigration Services (USCIS)

The U.S. petitioner and foreign fiancé(e) will both need the USCIS site:

- https://www.uscis.gov/

This site provides the following:

- List of all government forms: https://www.uscis.gov/forms
- Tracking the I-129F petition of the U.S. petitioner
- Tracking foreign fiancé(e)/spouse permanent residency card (green card)
- Official news from the USCIS
- Provides important information such as where the U.S. petitioner sends the package:

The USCIS Dallas Lockbox
For U.S. Postal Service:
USCIS
P.O. Box 660151
Dallas, TX 75266

For Express mail and courier deliveries:
USCIS
Attn: I-129F
2501 South State Highway 121 Business
Suite 400
Lewisville, TX 75067

Find a Local USCIS Immigration Office:
https://www.uscis.gov/about-us/find-uscis-office

U.S. State Department

The State Department works with foreign nationals to get them a visa to enter the US.
https://travel.state.gov/

- DS-160, Online Nonimmigrant Visa Application
  - https://ceac.state.gov/ceac/

- Use for tracking current visa status - Once the foreign fiancé(e) has had an embassy interview, they can check the status of their visa on travel.state.gov
- Contact to the **National Visa Center** will also be needed:
  - Used for getting your case number after I-129F approval
  - Call at (603) 334-0700
  - Email: NVCINQUIRY@state.gov
  - 32 Rochester Ave, Portsmouth, NH 03801
  - Department of State video: https://video.state.gov/

U.S. Embassy & Consulate

All embassies and consulates are under the U.S. State Department. Each embassy and consulate have their own contact information. Here is the main site for finding all the embassies and consulates:

- http://ustraveldocs.com

Other Government Agencies You May Need

U.S. Customs and Border Protection (CBP) - For questions about immigrants & nonimmigrants traveling outside the U.S. during the K-1 or green card process, the CBP may be a good resource.

- https://www.cbp.gov/
- Call at 1-800-877-8339

Social Security Administration (SSA) - When the immigrant gets a social security number, they will need to go to the local Social Security Administration office. Contacting the SSA may also be necessary if the U.S. petitioner needs to get evidence of receiving retirement or disability payments from the SSA.

- https://www.ssa.gov

County Clerk - The couple will need to contact the local county clerk's office (local town/city/county government) to get a marriage license and/or marriage certificate.

Forums & Social Media

Visajourney.com - They have additional guidance on visas, timelines. The most useful thing about the site is the community on the forum. You can search for just about any situation on K-1 and K2 visa and someone has had it happen.

immihelp.com/forum/ - On this forum people discuss many kinds of visas.

USCIS Facebook: https://www.facebook.com/uscis

USCIS twitter: https://twitter.com/uscis

USCIS Instagram: https://www.instagram.com/uscis/

USCIS Youtube: https://www.youtube.com/user/uscis

Department of State Facebook: https://www.facebook.com/usdos/

Department of State twitter: https://twitter.com/StateDept

Department of State Instagram: https://www.instagram.com/statedept

Department of State Youtube: https://www.youtube.com/user/statevideo

Visa Approved Facebook group (by Yuri & Bruce) - https://www.facebook.com/groups/k1visaAos

YuriBruce - https://www.facebook.com/teamyuribruce

Fiance Visa to USA! course - http://visaapproved.thinktific.com

Glossary

There are a few terms and acronyms that you will see over and over again throughout your process. We will just cover a few that you really need to know.

Alien - a legal alien is a non-citizen who is legally permitted to remain in a country. This is a very broad category which includes tourists, guest workers, legal permanent residents, and student visa resident aliens.

A-Number - An A-Number, also known as an Alien Registration Number or Alien Number, is a unique eight- or nine-digit number assigned to a noncitizen at the time their A-File is created.

Beneficiary - For the K-1, the beneficiary is the foreign fiancé(e) and the children. This is the applicant named by the U.S. petitioner in the I-129F.

Case Number - Once the National Visa Center gets an approved I-129F package, they assign a unique identifier (called a case number) and send it to the proper U.S. embassy (based on information provided in the I-129F). Once the petitioner gets the NOA2, they need to contact the National Visa Center and get the case number.

Certificate of No Marriage (CENOMAR) - Other names of the CENOMAR include a certificate of No Impediment, Single Statement, No Marital Certificate, Negative Statement of Marriage. U.S. embassy may or may not require this type of this document. Certificate of No Marriage is an official document proving that a foreign fiancé(e) is single.

Consulate - Official representative of the government of a country. An embassy is where an ambassador is based. A consulate does not have an ambassador. They do most of the basic services for citizens of their respective country and potential immigrants.

DHS - Department of Homeland Security (DHS) is the parent organization of U.S. Citizenship and Immigration Services (USCIS).

DOS - Department of State (DOS) is the federal organization that controls U.S embassies and consulates.

Executive Office for Immigration Review (EOIR) - The primary mission of the Executive Office for Immigration Review (EOIR) is to adjudicate immigration cases by fairly, expeditiously, and uniformly interpreting and administering the Nation's immigration laws.

IMB - International Marriage Broker operates largely online and invites male customers to review profiles of women living overseas in order to facilitate a marriage.

Immigrant - a person who comes to live permanently in a foreign country.

K-1 visa - K-1 is in the k-visa category for a fiancé(e) of U.S. citizens and their accompanying minor children. K-1 and K-2 visas were created to speed up the immigration process for such individuals, so they could travel more quickly to the United States.

K-2 visa - K-2 is in the K- visa category for minor children of a fiancé(e) of U.S. citizens.

K-3 visa - K-3 is the k-visa category for spouses of U.S citizens. If the U.S citizen is already married to a foreign national and wants to get a visa for their spouse, they need a K-3. K-4 is for the children of the foreign national spouse.

NBI - National Bureau of Investigation (Philippines) used to check criminal records or verify that there is no criminal record.

NVC - National Visa Center (NVC) in Portsmouth, New Hampshire does visa pre-processing. NVC is under the Department of State.

NOA - Notice of Action (NOA) is the name of the I-797 form.

NOA1 - is the very first letter that the USCIS will send to the petitioner. It contains a receipt number.

NOA2 - the second letter that the USCIS will send to the petitioner. It contains a rejection or approval and instructions on what to do next.

Nonimmigrant - An alien who seeks temporary entry to the United States for a specific purpose. The alien must have a permanent residence abroad (for most classes of admission) and qualify for the nonimmigrant classification sought.

Nonimmigrant visa - A nonimmigrant visa is the visa issued to a person with a permanent residence outside the U.S. but who wishes to be in the U.S on a temporary basis (i.e. Tourism, medical treatment, business, temporary work, or study). A K-1 visa is a nonimmigrant visa; however, it allows the beneficiary to adjust status in the U.S.

Notice of Action - Notice of Action is the name of the I-797 form.

Petitioner - The person who submits the initial request to USCIS, which upon approval, will allow the foreign national to submit a visa application. The foreign national would be the beneficiary.

POE - Port of Entry (POE) refers to what airport the traveler will arrive in the destination country. For the US, it is the very first soil of the state you step in.

RFE - Request for more Evidence (RFE) is when USCIS or DOS requires more information to move forward in the visa process.

USCIS - United States Citizenship and Immigration Services (USCIS) is a component of the United States Department of Homeland Security (DHS).

U.S. Embassy - U.S. embassies and consulates abroad, as well as foreign embassies and consulates in the United States, have a special status. The primary purpose of an embassy is to assist American citizens who travel to or live in the host country.

Forms

Form I-129f, Petition for Alien Fiancé(e) - The form that the U.S. petitioner needs to fill out to request a temporary "K" visa for their spouse or fiancé(e). A married couple files for a K-3 and an engaged couple files for a K-1. This form is accompanied by supporting documents that prove evidence of an ongoing relationship, intent to marry, U.S. citizenship, meeting in person, and other requirements (https://www.uscis.gov/i-129f).

G-235A, Biographical Information (NO LONGER USED) - The biographical information has been integrated into the I-129F.

G-1145, eNotification of Application - This form is used to request a text message and/or email when USCIS accepts your form (https://www.uscis.gov/g-1145).

G-1450, Authorization for Credit Card Transactions - Use this form to pay fees for any form processed at a USCIS Lockbox. There is no additional fee to pay with your credit card (https://www.uscis.gov/g-1450).

G-28, Notice of Entry of Appearance - Used to provide information on your eligibility to act on behalf of an applicant, petitioner, or respondent. Used by attorneys or accredited representative (https://www.uscis.gov/g-28).

G-28I, Notice of Entry of Appearance as Attorney in Matters Outside the Geographical Confines of the United States - To provide notice that an attorney admitted to the practice of the law in a country other than the United States seeks to appear before DHS in a matter outside the geographical confines of the United States.

I-797, Notice of Action (approval) - USCIS issues this form when it approves an application or a petition that it received. This is commonly known as the application approval notice or NOA2. This form serves as proof of certain immigration benefits. Applicants should retain this notice as it is an important document.

I-797A, Notice of Action (I-94) - Issued to an applicant as a replacement Form I-94 (https://www.uscis.gov/i-797-info).

I-797B, Notice of Action (work) - Issued for approval of an alien worker petition (https://www.uscis.gov/i-797-info).

I-797C, Notice of Action (information) - Issued to communicate receipt of payments, rejection of applications, transfer of files, fingerprint biometric, interview and re-scheduled appointments, and re-open cases (https://www.uscis.gov/forms/form-i-797c-notice-action).

I-797D, Notice of Action (benefits) - Accompanies benefit cards (https://www.uscis.gov/i-797-info).

I-797E, Notice of Action (request evidence) - Issued to request evidence (https://www.uscis.gov/i-797-info).

I-797F, Transportation Letter - Issued overseas to allow applicants to travel (https://www.uscis.gov/i-797-info).

DS-160, Online Nonimmigrant Visa Application form - DS-160 is for temporary travel to the United States, and for K fiancé(e) visas. Form DS-160 is submitted electronically to the Department of State website via the Internet. Consular officers use the information entered on the DS-160 to process the visa application and, combined with a personal interview, determine an applicant's eligibility for a nonimmigrant visa (https://ceac.state.gov/genniv/).

I-485, Application Adjust Status - The foreign spouse uses this form to apply for lawful permanent resident status (green card) once in the United States (https://www.uscis.gov/i-485).

I-130, Petition for Alien Relatives - This form is for a U.S. citizen or lawful permanent resident of the United States who needs to establish their relationship to certain alien relatives who wish to immigrate to the United States (https://www.uscis.gov/i-130).

I-131, Application for Travel - Use this form to apply for a re-entry permit, refugee travel document, or advance parole travel document, to include parole into the U.S. for humanitarian reasons (https://www.uscis.gov/i-131).

I-9, Employment Eligibility Verification - Form I-9 is used for verifying the identity and employment authorization of individuals hired for employment in the United States. All U.S. employers must ensure proper completion of Form I-9 for everyone they hire for employment in the United States (https://www.uscis.gov/i-9).

I-94,   Arrival-Departure   Record   - (https://i94.cbp.dhs.gov/I94) a place for U.S. visitors to find travel records.

I-765, Application for Employment - Certain foreign nationals, who are eligible to work in the United States, use Form I-765 to request an employment authorization document (EAD) (https://www.uscis.gov/i-765).

I-864, Affidavit of Support (family) - Most family-based immigrants and some employment-based immigrants use this form to show they have adequate means of financial support and are not likely to rely on the U.S. government for financial support (https://www.uscis.gov/i-864).

I-90, Replace Permanent Resident Card - Use this form to replace a Green Card (https://www.uscis.gov/i-90).

I-156, Visa Application (NO LONGER USED) - Was used for the nonimmigrant visa application. This was replaced with DS-160.

Made in the USA
Columbia, SC
06 March 2022